# 100
## ENDANGERED
## SPECIES

# 100 ENDANGERED SPECIES

**RACHEL HUDSON**

Button
BOOKS

# Contents

Giant anteater
**16**

Aye-aye
**18**

Orangutan
**20**

Horned
marsupial frog
**22**

Southern
woolly lemur
**24**

Philippine
crocodile
**26**

Kakapo
**28**

Whale shark
**30**

Moscardón
**32**

Green turtle
**34**

Eurasian beaver
**36**

Javan warty pig
**38**

Persian leopard
**40**

Giant panda
**42**

Danube
clouded yellow
**44**

Tasmanian devil
**46**

Greater
one-horned rhino
**48**

Pygmy raccoon
**50**

Mountain hare
**52**

Ethiopian wolf
**54**

Parson's
chameleon
**56**

Sunda pangolin
**58**

African wild dog
**60**

Hazel dormouse
**62**

Spectacled bear
**64**

Whooping crane
**66**

Hedgehog seahorse
**68**

Purple-faced langur
**70**

Giant dragon lizard
**72**

Caspian seal
**74**

Reticulated giraffe
**76**

Red slender loris
**78**

Volcán Darwin giant tortoise
**80**

Red panda
**82**

Cheetah
**84**

Dhole
**86**

Asian elephant
**88**

Stag beetle
**90**

Rusty patched bumblebee
**92**

Malayan tapir
**94**

Andean flamingo
**96**

Horvath's toad-headed agama
**98**

Hawksbill turtle
**100**

Polar bear
**102**

White-winged nightjar
**104**

Pallas's cat
**106**

Variable harlequin frog
**108**

Bonobo
**110**

Lulworth skipper
**112**

African elephant
**114**

# Foreword

Who knew that Philippine crocodiles swallow stones to regulate their buoyancy? Or that the giant dragon lizard (opposite) was the inspiration for Smaug, the dragon in J.R.R. Tolkien's book, *The Hobbit*? I thoroughly enjoyed unearthing these and a host of other nuggets from the succinct and informative text in this inspiring book.

Rachel Hudson has a special talent for capturing the essence of each of her chosen species, and she portrays them with a twinkle in her eye – look at the aye-aye, feeling its way gingerly along a branch, or the blatant inquisitiveness of the giant otters.

There are surprises here, too. Rubbing shoulders with the giant panda and the orangutan are the sea aster mining bee and the pygmy raccoon. Sadly, the variety of animals is matched by the many threats they face, but it is heartening to read about the vital work that so many people and organizations are doing to protect them. In case we are in any doubt about the need for action, the baiji (or Chinese river dolphin) is a sharp reminder that extinction is forever. I sincerely hope that this book will spur you on to play your part in preventing further losses.

*Brett Westwood, naturalist and broadcaster*
*October 2020*

# Introduction

This little book has a BIG ambition: to highlight 100 endangered species and the incredible work being done to save them. From panda bears to Patagonian bumblebees, this book introduces you to some very special characters of all shapes and sizes. They range from the charismatic to the feared, the persecuted to the overlooked.

Over thousands of years, each of these 100 species has evolved to adapt to its environment, from the frozen North and arid desert, to lush rainforests and tropical seas. Many play a vital role as an engineer, gardener, or caretaker of their neighborhood, creating new habitat, dispersing seeds, pollinating or tidying up. A few are top of their food web, helping to keep a balance among other animals. Some are indicator species, telling us how healthy a habitat really is. Losing any one of these species may have serious consequences for their entire ecosystem and a host of other plants and animals, including us.

Alongside fascinating facts, you will learn about the plight of these species and the threats they face. A recurring theme will be

their need for a safe place to call home. You can also find out how local people are providing solutions and what organizations are doing to help. Towards the end of the book, you'll discover a list of website addresses for these organizations, which will provide more information and advice on how you can get involved.

This book is intended for all nature lovers, from the curious to the concerned. I became hooked on wildlife at the age of seven, when I joined my local Watch Club. I went on to work for a conservation charity and today, as a freelance illustrator, I am thrilled to be working with many of the leading nature conservation organizations in the UK. *100 Endangered Species* began as a collaboration with the People's Trust for Endangered Species. For 100 days I illustrated one species a day, to highlight the work of the Trust, and posted it on social media. Since then, this book has evolved to include other organizations and the animals they are working tirelessly to protect.

I may have chosen to focus on these particular species, but this book is ultimately a celebration of the variety of life on our planet.

# How this book works

Every one of the 100 species in this book is on the International Union
for the Conservation of Nature's (IUCN) Red List, which was established
in 1964. This is the world's most comprehensive and up-to-date source
of information on the status of animal and plant species threatened
with extinction. It is a critical indicator of the health of the world's
biodiversity and a powerful tool to inform conservation action and
policy change.

The IUCN Red List uses nine categories of classification to indicate
the increasing risk of global extinction, of which we feature seven
(see below). Whether species are classified as being Least Concern,
Vulnerable or Critically Endangered, they are on the Red List because
they are all in trouble. Every one of the 100 entries in the book is
a conservation priority.

An arrow indicates the Red List status of each species, and the
corresponding color is then used on the accompanying map. For
example, the diagram below indicates a status of Endangered:

## *Red List Classification*

| Extinct | Threatened | Lower Risk |
|---|---|---|
| EX: Extinct | CR: Critically Endangered | NT: Near Threatened |
| EW: Extinct in the Wild | EN: Endangered | LC: Least Concern |
| | VU: Vulnerable | |

## Location

## Information

| | |
|---|---|
| Population trend | **Decreasing** |
| Habitats | **Forest, grassland** |
| Distribution | **India, Southeast Asia** |
| Threats | **Habitat loss, conflict, wildlife trade** |

Each entry includes a globe, which shows where the species can be found in the world, and the patterned background corresponds to the place they call their home. There is also a table that lists population trend, habitats, distribution, and the main threats faced by that species.

The illustrations are accompanied by written descriptions, which combine fascinating facts with a focus on why the species is at risk. Wherever possible, there is a summary of current conservation actions attempting to understand and address the specific threats. Turn to the back of the book to find website addresses for organizations and initiatives that are working to prevent extinctions and maintain the world's precious diversity.

| | |
|---|---|
| Population trend | **Decreasing** |
| Habitats | **Forest, grassland, savanna, shrubland** |
| Distribution | **Central and South America** |
| Threats | **Habitat loss, deforestation, hunting, fire, persecution** |

# Giant anteater

*Myrmecophaga tridactyla*

The giant anteater is the largest of the four anteater species. It has a long, tube-shaped nose with a tiny mouth, no teeth, and a very long, sticky tongue, which is perfect for vacuuming up thousands of insects, especially ants and termites. Giant anteaters wander in a wide variety of habitats, from tropical forest to open savanna. They are now the most threatened mammals in Central America because they have lost their homes to deforestation and are one of the most common species to be killed on roads in Brazil. Many giant anteaters live in the Cerrado, the largest savanna in South America, but it's being cleared faster than the Amazon rainforest, and previously inaccessible areas are becoming exposed, as dirt roads are transformed into highways.

To give giant anteaters a better chance of survival, conservationists are carrying out research to develop landscape and road management guidelines. They are tackling illegal hunting and working on reintroduction programs in areas such as the Corrientes province in Argentina.

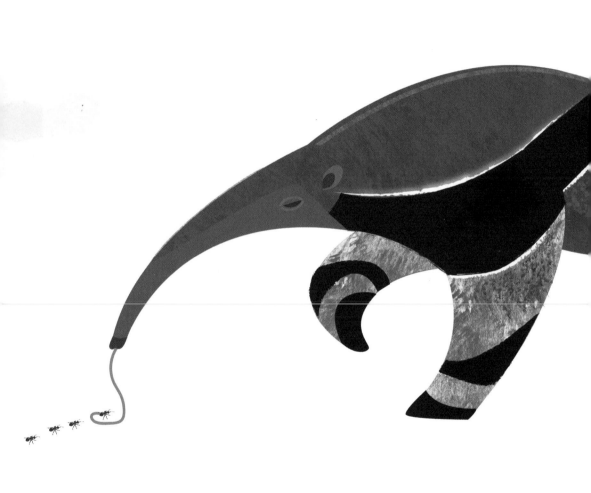

| | |
|---:|:---|
| Population trend | **Decreasing** |
| Habitats | **Forest, shrubland** |
| Distribution | **Madagascar** |
| Threats | **Habitat loss, deforestation, hunting, fire, persecution** |

EX EW CR **EN** VU NT LC

# Aye-aye
*Daubentonia madagascariensis*

With its large ears, rodent-like teeth, and extra-long, thin middle finger, the aye-aye once defied classification. It is, in fact, a lemur and the world's largest nocturnal primate. At night, it climbs trees and taps on the bark with its skinny middle finger. If the bark sounds hollow, the aye-aye uses its amazing hearing to pinpoint the wood-boring insect grubs inside the tree. Then, using its powerful front teeth, it rips open the bark and uses its middle finger to hook out the grubs. Many people native to Madagascar consider the aye-aye to be an evil omen and some believe that it can curse a person simply by pointing at them. As a consequence, when they are found they are often killed immediately. Hunting and habitat destruction have also put aye-aye populations at risk.

Today, the aye-aye is protected by law, and many organizations are working hard to preserve what's left of the forest where it lives. Captive breeding programs are attempting to boost the population and bridges have been constructed to link parts of the forest now divided by roads.

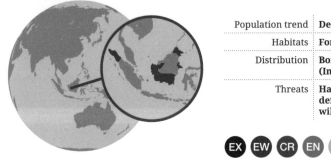

| | |
|---|---|
| Population trend | **Decreasing** |
| Habitats | **Forest** |
| Distribution | **Borneo, Sumatra (Indonesia)** |
| Threats | **Habitat loss, deforestation, hunting, wildlife trade** |

EX  EW  CR  EN  VU  NT  LC
▲

# Orangutan

*Pongo abelii, Pongo pygmaeus* and *Pongo tapanuliensis*

In Malay, orangutan means "person of the forest," and this gentle giant is one of our closest relatives. With long, powerful arms and grasping hands and feet, orangutans are perfectly adapted to life among the branches. They feed mainly on wild fruits, but will also eat honey and even birds' eggs. Among the most adept of tool users, they construct elaborate nests each night to sleep in. Orangutans play a vital role in the health of the rainforest ecosystem, dispersing seeds in their droppings, enabling plants to germinate and grow. Illegal logging, oil palm plantations, forest fires, and mining are all contributing to the catastrophic destruction of their home. Poachers are also killing mother orangutans to sell their babies as pets.

Conservationists are working with local communities to protect the forest and promote research and education. They are calling for palm oil companies to grow native plants alongside crops, and campaigning for animal trafficking to be better policed. Orangutans that have been kept illegally as pets are being released into the wild in Sumatra as part of a reintroduction program.

| | |
|---:|:---|
| Population trend | **Decreasing** |
| Habitats | **Forest, wetlands** |
| Distribution | **Colombia, Costa Rica, Ecuador, Panama** |
| Threats | **Habitat loss, climate change, disease** |

EX EW CR **EN** VU NT LC

# Horned marsupial frog

*Gastrotheca cornuta*

The horned marsupial frog is active at night in the tropical forests of Panama, Costa Rica, and Ecuador, and the lowland forests of Colombia. High up in the tree canopy, the male calls for a mate, sounding very much like a champagne cork being popped. Part of the family of marsupial frogs, the female carries her eggs in a pouch on her back, and they later hatch as fully formed froglets, rather than tadpoles. The eggs of this species are the largest known amphibian eggs. These frogs are disappearing fast. One cause is habitat loss through farming, the building of roads, oil palm plantations, and drilling and mining operations. The climate crisis and a parasitic disease may also be to blame.

Organizations, such as the World Land Trust, are supporting conservation projects in Columbia and Ecuador to protect the tropical forest habitat for this frog and a range of other endangered species.

| | |
|---:|:---|
| Population trend | **Unknown** |
| Habitats | **Forest** |
| Distribution | **Southeast Madagascar** |
| Threats | **Habitat loss, deforestation** |

# Southern woolly lemur

*Avahi meridionalis*

At night, in the coastal forests of southeast Madagascar, the southern woolly lemur is picking its way through the trees in search of tasty buds and leaves. In between meals, it will take long naps to digest its food. This lemur lives in small groups of two to five animals, often made up of parents and several generations of their offspring. Human activities, such as slash-and-burn agriculture, are causing their forest home and the animals that live in it to be severely at risk. Southern woolly lemurs are already listed as Endangered, so their shrinking habitat is cause for alarm.

The region's rich variety of wildlife has attracted conservation charities and scientific researchers for many years. They are continuing to learn more about this species and its ecosystem, which will help them to develop much-needed conservation programs.

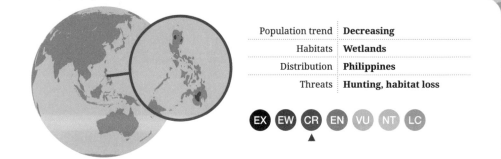

| | |
|---:|:---|
| Population trend | **Decreasing** |
| Habitats | **Wetlands** |
| Distribution | **Philippines** |
| Threats | **Hunting, habitat loss** |

EX EW **CR** EN VU NT LC
▲

# Philippine crocodile

*Crocodylus mindorensis*

The small freshwater Philippine crocodile has a broad snout and thick, bony plates along its back. It lives in ponds, marshes, and small rivers, and can change the color of its skin to match its surroundings. During the day, these crocodiles rest in the sun to warm up. When they are too hot they open their mouths to release heat. They are able to float on the water's surface, swallowing stones to control their buoyancy. These crocodiles are highly regarded by the indigenous people of the Philippines, but not so much by the rest of the population. They are feared, so they are killed. However, their aggressive image isn't deserved: they don't attack humans, unless provoked. This, and loss of habitat, has led them to become the most severely threatened crocodile species in the world.

Conservationists are working hard to change people's perception of the Philippine crocodile, which is now protected by law, and are running captive breeding and reintroduction programs.

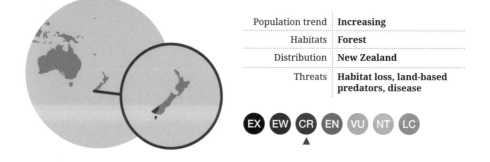

| | |
|---:|:---|
| Population trend | **Increasing** |
| Habitats | **Forest** |
| Distribution | **New Zealand** |
| Threats | **Habitat loss, land-based predators, disease** |

EX  EW  **CR**  EN  VU  NT  LC

# Kakapo
*Strigops habroptila*

The kakapo is the world's only flightless parrot. Large and rotund, it is also the heaviest. Since it is nocturnal and has a striking facial disc, it also goes by the name of "owl parrot." Kakapos move around with a waddling walk and freeze when startled in an attempt to blend into the background. They climb trees and come back down to earth by using their small wings as a parachute. Kakapos were once widespread in New Zealand, but were heavily hunted for their meat and feathers; friendly in nature, they were easy to catch. The rats, cats, and stoats that humans brought with them to the islands also annihilated these birds, their chicks, and their eggs.

Since the launch of the Kakapo Recovery program in the 1980s, these birds have been kept on three remote predator-free islands. There are feeding stations for the birds, and their nests are monitored. Sometimes, eggs are artificially incubated and chicks are hand-reared.

| | |
|---|---|
| Population trend | **Decreasing** |
| Habitats | **Marine** |
| Distribution | **Worldwide (except Mediterranean Sea)** |
| Threats | **Bycatch, poaching, pollution, climate change, vessel strikes** |

EX  EW  CR  **EN**  VU  NT  LC

# Whale shark

*Rhincodon typus*

These slow-moving, gentle giants are not in fact whales, but the world's largest fish, growing up to 40 feet (12 meters) long. Each shark is covered in a unique pattern of spots and stripes. Inside its huge mouth are long, comb-like structures, known as gill rakers, which trap and filter plankton, small fish, and krill. Whale sharks are migratory, traveling vast distances and often returning to the same locations each year. Their presence indicates a healthy ocean with plentiful plankton. They face a number of threats, not least getting tangled in fishing nets and being hunted for their fins. Whale sharks can be injured in collisions with boats, and, as filter feeders, they sometimes swallow plastic. Global heating is warming the world's oceans and this has an effect on whale shark numbers, their habitats, and their prey.

Marine conservationists are closely monitoring populations and working with local communities to improve whale shark tourism.

| | |
|---|---|
| Population trend | **Decreasing** |
| Habitats | **Forest** |
| Distribution | **Argentina, Chile** |
| Threats | **Disease, competition, habitat degradation** |

EX EW CR **EN** VU NT LC
▲

# Moscardón

*Bombus dahlbomii*

This Patagonian bee, also known as the "flying mouse," is the world's biggest bumblebee. It bobs its way through the temperate forests of Chile and Argentina. It is hugely respected by the indigenous Mapuche people, as they believe it carries the spirit of the dead. It is an important pollinator of native plants, especially those in isolated areas. With its long tongue it can feed on deep flowers, such as the Chilean bellflower. The dramatic decline of this species is thought to be due to disease spread by European bees, which were introduced to South America to pollinate crops. Commercial bees also compete with wild bees for food, invade new habitats, and upset the balance of plant species.

It is now illegal to import any kind of bumblebee from overseas into the United States, but not South America. Scientists and bee conservationists are calling for the European Union to ban the export of all bumblebees.

| Population trend | **Decreasing** |
| --- | --- |
| Habitats | **Marine** |
| Distribution | **Atlantic, Indian and Pacific Oceans** |
| Threats | **Over-exploitation, poaching of eggs, bycatch, plastic pollution, disease, climate change** |

EX EW CR **EN** VU NT LC
▲

# Green turtle

*Chelonia mydas*

Gliding through tropical waters, these large herbivores spend their days grazing on seagrasses and algae. Caretakers of the ocean, green turtles keep the seagrass ecosystem healthy, which is vital for young invertebrates and fish to thrive. They travel vast distances between feeding and nesting grounds, in search of a safe beach to lay their eggs. Suitable nesting sites are becoming scarce because of development and tourism. When they do find a beach and lay their eggs, people often harvest them before they hatch and sell them as food. Out at sea, adult turtles are hunted for their meat and shells, or become trapped in fishing gear.

Conservationists are encouraging governments to strengthen laws to protect sea turtles and their habitats. They are working with fisheries to help them reduce bycatch and switch to more turtle-friendly fishing equipment. In the Turks and Caicos Islands, legislation to ensure all turtle fishing is sustainable has been approved.

| | |
|---|---|
| Population trend | **Increasing** |
| Habitats | **Forest, shrubland, wetlands** |
| Distribution | **Asia, Europe** |
| Threats | **Overhunting, roadkill, competition, habitat loss** |

EX EW CR EN VU NT **LC**
▲

# Eurasian beaver

*Castor fiber*

One of the largest members of the rodent family, the beaver has a thick, brown fur coat, a broad, flattened tail, and huge orange teeth. Using its tail as a rudder, the beaver is an expert swimmer and can stay underwater for up to six minutes. It feeds on aquatic plants and grasses, as well as bark, twigs, and leaves. An architect of the animal world, it transforms the local environment by building dams and creating new wetland homes for other wildlife, from fish to fungi. Beaver dams can also reduce flood risk, increase water storage and improve water quality. In the UK, these industrious rodents were hunted to extinction during the 16th century.

Following successful reintroductions, there are now wild, free-ranging beavers in Scotland, France, southern Germany and Austria. In 2016, the Scottish population was formally recognised as a native species, but they are not yet protected by law.

| | |
|---:|:---|
| Population trend | **Decreasing** |
| Habitats | **Forest** |
| Distribution | **Java (Indonesia)** |
| Threats | **Hunting, habitat loss, conflict, competition** |

EX EW CR **EN** VU NT LC
▲

# Javan warty pig

*Sus verrucosus*

The Javan warty pig lives on the most populated island in the world, located in Indonesia's Java Sea. It spends its nights foraging for roots and tubers in small pockets of rainforest and forest gardens cultivated by local villagers. A typical male has three pairs of large warts on each side of its face. Restricted to just a few isolated places, this species has shown a rapid population decline in recent decades. Farming is the greatest threat to these pigs, with farmers often killing those caught raiding their crops. They are also killed by sport hunters, who see the animal as a trophy. European wild pigs also live on the island and compete with warty pigs for habitat and food.

Conservationists are working with the local community to raise awareness and find ways to protect crops without harming the island's wildlife.

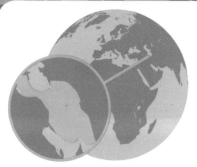

| | |
|---|---|
| Population trend | **Decreasing** |
| Habitats | **Mountain, forest** |
| Distribution | **Afghanistan, Iran, Pakistan, Western Turkey** |
| Threats | **Habitat loss, hunting, decline in prey** |

EX EW CR EN VU NT LC
▲

# Persian leopard

*Panthera pardus tulliana*

The Persian leopard, also known as the Caucasian leopard, prefers its own company in distant mountainous regions, ranging from arid areas to dense forest and snow-capped peaks. It will travel far in search of gazelle, roe deer, and wild boar. It is an ambush hunter and will lie on the ground, creeping up to within three feet (one meter) of potential prey before pouncing. Persian leopards face a variety of threats, including housing developments, livestock farming, hunting, and trapping. These big cats roam across multiple protected areas, often crossing international borders, making conservation work a particular challenge. The world population is estimated at fewer than 1,300 mature individuals, and it's continuing to decline.

International conservation organizations are trying to ensure national parks with Persian leopards are protected. They are working with communities, sharing their findings, and carrying out reintroduction programs.

| | |
|---|---|
| Population trend | **Increasing** |
| Habitats | **Forest** |
| Distribution | **Central China** |
| Threats | **Habitat loss, poaching** |

**EX** **EW** **CR** **EN** **VU** **NT** **LC**
▲

# Giant panda

*Ailuropoda melanoleuca*

The solitary giant panda has become an international symbol for nature conservation. It is represented in the logo for the World Wildlife Fund (WWF), which was established in 1961. In deep thickets of bamboo forest in central China, the panda's bold black-and-white coloring provides camouflage. In this cool, wet habitat, the panda spends 12 hours a day eating the leaves, shoots, and stems of bamboo. As a result of farming, deforestation, and other development, the giant panda has been driven out of the lowland areas where it once lived. Fewer than 1,900 pandas are thought to remain in the wild.

The WWF has been helping the Chinese government with its National Conservation Program for the giant panda and its habitat. Thanks to this program, panda reserves now cover more than 3.8 million acres of bamboo forest. Wild panda numbers are finally increasing, and in 2016, their Endangered status was reclassified as Vulnerable.

| Population trend | **Decreasing** |
| --- | --- |
| Habitats | **Forest, grassland** |
| Distribution | **Central and Eastern Europe** |
| Threats | **Habitat loss, intensive agriculture, climate change** |

EX EW CR **EN** VU NT LC

# Danube clouded yellow

*Colias myrmidone*

The Danube clouded yellow is one of the fastest-disappearing European butterfly species. It is a large, vibrant-yellow butterfly once found along much of the River Danube, from Germany to Romania and Russia. Unlike most other butterflies, the Danube clouded yellow's wings are not always mirror images, making it better at hiding in fields of flowers. It usually rests with its wings closed. To thrive, this butterfly needs a patchwork of warm, traditionally managed meadows, pastures, open forests, and woodland edges, which are found along the forest-steppes running from central Europe to western Siberia. They are classified as Endangered as their traditionally managed habitats disappear due to more intensive farming.

The Danube clouded yellow is protected by the European Habitats Directive. It needs more wildlife-rich farmland to be created in order to survive. In Russia, local children are learning about the need to preserve butterfly havens and the grasslands that they favor through special butterfly clubs.

| | |
|---:|:---|
| Population trend | **Decreasing** |
| Habitats | **Forest, shrubland, grassland, caves** |
| Distribution | **Tasmania (Australia)** |
| Threats | **Disease, roadkill, persecution** |

EX  EW  CR  **EN**  VU  NT  LC
▲

# Tasmanian devil

*Sarcophilus harrisii*

The Tasmanian devil is a small, stocky marsupial, famous for its feisty attitude. It is only found in Australia's island state of Tasmania. Covered in black fur with a white band across its chest, it has a large head and ears that flush red. It is a useful "vacuum cleaner" of the forest, roaming long distances at night to feed on dead carcasses. It also preys on feral cats and foxes that would otherwise devastate native wildlife. It is during communal feeding that the devil may fly into a rage, displaying its wide jaws and snarling to ward off threats. The greatest threat to this animal is a contagious cancer believed to be transmitted from devil to devil through biting. Facial tumours prevent them from feeding, leading to starvation.

There are various strategies underway to combat the spread of the disease, including population isolation, disease suppression, selection for resistance, and vaccine research. The Save the Tasmanian Devil Program has established a disease-free population on Tasmania's Maria Island and collaborates with researchers and zoos across the world.

| | |
|---:|:---|
| Population trend | **Increasing** |
| Habitats | **Forest, grassland** |
| Distribution | **Nepal, Northern India** |
| Threats | **Poaching, habitat loss** |

EX EW CR EN VU NT LC
▲

# Greater one-horned rhino

*Rhinoceros unicornis*

The single black horn of this rhinoceros has led to its brilliant Latin name, *Rhinoceros unicornis*. It is the largest of the rhino species and traipses through the world's tallest grasslands in northern India and Nepal. It is a grazing animal, with a diet almost entirely consisting of grasses, as well as the leaves and branches of shrubs and trees, fruit, and aquatic plants. The droppings of Indian rhinos are essential in the dispersal, germination, and fertilizing of seeds, so that trees can colonize new areas. Despite their protection, they are still poached for their horns. There are fewer than 3,000 animals remaining in the wild.

The majority of these rhinos live in Kaziranga National Park in India. While poaching is an ongoing problem there, rhino numbers have increased as a direct result of conservation work carried out by organizations such as the People's Trust for Endangered Species.

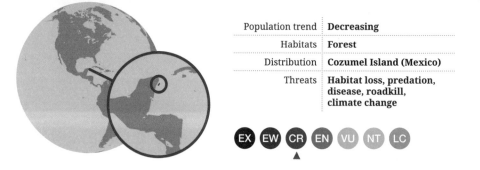

| | |
|---:|:---|
| Population trend | **Decreasing** |
| Habitats | **Forest** |
| Distribution | **Cozumel Island (Mexico)** |
| Threats | **Habitat loss, predation, disease, roadkill, climate change** |

EX  EW  **CR**  EN  VU  NT  LC

# Pygmy raccoon
*Procyon pygmaeus*

The pygmy raccoon is half the size of its American cousin, has shorter fur and a yellow tint to its tail. It is only found on Cozumel Island, off the Yucatán Peninsula in Mexico. Close to the water, among mangrove thickets and sandy wetlands, it will search for its main source of food: mangrove crabs. During the wet season, when these are less abundant, it switches to fruit and vegetation. Restricted to just one part of their small island home, pygmy raccoons have no escape from rising sea levels, which are being caused by the climate crisis. They are losing habitat to development from the tourism industry. They also fall prey to non-native predators, which bring disease with them. There are only 300 pygmy raccoons left in the wild.

Two protected areas have been created on Cozumel since 2010, which cover almost half of the island. Initiatives are underway for public education and the removal of non-native predators.

| | |
|---:|:---|
| Population trend | **Stable** |
| Habitats | **Forest, shrubland, grassland, wetlands** |
| Distribution | **Asia, Europe** |
| Threats | **Habitat loss, roadkill, hunting, climate change** |

EX  EW  CR  EN  VU  NT  **LC**
▲

# Mountain hare

*Lepus timidus*

The mountain hare is known for its camouflage. In summer, it has a gray-brown coat with a blueish tinge to match its heathland habitat. In winter, it turns white to blend in with a snowy backdrop – only the tips of its ears stay black. They are larger than rabbits, but smaller than brown hares and have shorter ears. They graze on grasses and heather, and nibble leaves and twigs. When disturbed, they zigzag across the moors, using their muscular hind legs to power them forward. Mountain hares died out in England during the last Ice Age, but were reintroduced in the 1800s in the Scottish Highlands and the Peak District. They are now facing modern threats, including road traffic and global heating. They are also culled to control their numbers as part of game and hunting management.

UK conservation organizations are restoring and protecting heathlands and calling for a halt to the culling of mountain hares. The species is protected in small areas across Europe.

| Population trend | **Decreasing** |
| --- | --- |
| Habitats | **Shrubland, grassland, wetlands, rocky areas** |
| Distribution | **Ethiopia** |
| Threats | **Habitat loss, conflict, disease** |

EX EW CR **EN** VU NT LC

# Ethiopian wolf

*Canis simensis*

The Ethiopian wolf is the rarest member of the canid family, which is made up of dogs, wolves, and foxes. It has long legs, a narrow muzzle, a distinctive rust-colored coat, and a bushy tail. It is found only in the highlands of Ethiopia and is Africa's most threatened carnivore. Ethiopian wolves live in close-knit territorial packs, typically made up of an extended family group. All adults will help to care for pups by feeding and protecting them. There are, however, fewer than 440 wolves left in the wild. Humans pose the largest threat, with human subsistence farming rapidly swallowing their habitat. They are now restricted to a few isolated enclaves in the highlands.

The Ethiopian Wolf Conservation Program is a partnership between the University of Oxford's Wildlife Conservation Research Unit (WildCRU) and the Born Free Foundation, and supports conservation, monitoring, and management of these wolves, as well as disease prevention and control through vaccination campaigns.

| | |
|---:|:---|
| Population trend | **Decreasing** |
| Habitats | **Forest** |
| Distribution | **Madagascar** |
| Threats | **Habitat loss, wildlife trade** |

# Parson's chameleon
*Calumma parsonii*

The Parson's chameleon is one of the world's largest chameleons and can reach a length of 28 inches (70 centimeters). It is one of more than 80 species of chameleon (half of the world's total) found only on the island of Madagascar. With fused toes and a strong tail used for gripping, this reptile is perfectly adapted to life in the treetops. To capture its prey, it shoots out its long, sticky tongue and uses it as a suction cup. The chameleon's impressive rainbow of skin colors conveys emotions, such as anger or fear, and provides camouflage. The population of Parson's chameleon has declined by 20 percent in less than two decades. This is mainly due to habitat loss, driven by slash-and-burn agriculture and logging, and the wildlife trade.

To help Parson's chameleons to recover, strict rules have been established in Madagascar to control the export of this species to be sold as pets.

| | |
|---|---|
| Population trend | **Decreasing** |
| Habitats | **Forest, shrubland** |
| Distribution | **Southeast Asia** |
| Threats | **Hunting, poaching, wildlife trade, habitat loss** |

EX EW **CR** EN VU NT LC
▲

# Sunda pangolin

*Manis javanica*

Pangolins, or scaly anteaters, are mammals covered in hard scales made of keratin. At night, they feed on ants and termites, using their claws to rip open nests and a long, thin, sticky tongue to scoop up the insects. The word "pangolin" is derived from the Malay word *penggulung*, meaning "roller," a reference to the way in which pangolins roll up into a ball when they feel threatened. Unfortunately, they are one of the most heavily poached and exploited animals in the world. They are hunted for their skin, scales, and meat, which are used for clothing and traditional medicine. Despite being protected almost everywhere in their range, illegal international trade has led to Sunda pangolins being classified as Critically Endangered.

With international support, anti-poaching patrols and law enforcement are being established at key sites. Conservationists are trying to reduce the demand for pangolin products in China and are working with local communities to develop more sustainable livelihoods.

| | |
|---:|:---|
| Population trend | **Decreasing** |
| Habitats | **Forest, savanna, shrubland, grassland, desert** |
| Distribution | **Sub-Saharan Africa** |
| Threats | **Habitat loss, conflict** |

EX EW CR **EN** VU NT LC

# African wild dog

*Lycaon pictus*

African wild dogs, or painted dogs, roam the open plains and sparse woodlands of sub-Saharan Africa. Each animal's mottled coat, made up of irregular patches of red, black, brown, and yellow, is unique. They have big, rounded ears and four toes on each foot, unlike other dogs, which have five toes on their front feet. They are highly intelligent and hunt in cooperative packs to prey on gazelle, antelope, and wildebeest. These dogs are in steady decline due to their shrinking habitat. As human settlements expand and farming intensifies, African wild dogs sometimes venture into developed areas and attack livestock. This often results in retaliatory killings by farmers.

To reduce the number of attacks on livestock, project workers are helping local communities to build enclosures, or bomas, and an outreach program aims to improve the public perception of these dogs at all levels of society. Wild dog movements are also monitored to anticipate and prevent potential conflict with humans.

| | |
|---|---|
| Population trend | **Unknown** |
| Habitats | **Forest** |
| Distribution | **Europe** |
| Threats | **Habitat loss, intensive agriculture, climate change** |

EX EW CR EN VU NT LC
▲

# Hazel dormouse

*Muscardinus avellanarius*

Also known as the common dormouse, the hazel dormouse can be easily recognised by its fluffy tail, and spends nearly three-quarters of the year asleep. From fall to spring, it hibernates in a leafy nest on the forest floor or in the base of hedgerows. It spends the summer in the branches of trees. Once widespread across Britain, it is already extinct in many counties in England, hanging on mostly in southern parts of England and Wales. National monitoring shows the population has halved since 2000. Changes in woodland management, farming practices and loss of hedgerows have all taken a heavy toll on their living space, as well as the climate crisis.

Dormice are a protected species in Britain and regarded as a priority for conservation action. Through monitoring, reintroducing dormice to well-managed woodland, and training woodland managers, conservationists are trying to bring them back to the places where they've been lost.

| | |
|---|---|
| Population trend | **Decreasing** |
| Habitats | **Forest, grassland, scrubland** |
| Distribution | **Bolivia, Colombia, Ecuador, Peru, Venezuela** |
| Threats | **Habitat loss, intensive agriculture, hunting, climate change** |

EX EW CR EN **VU** NT LC
▲

# Spectacled bear

*Tremarctos ornatus*

The story of Paddington Bear is based on the spectacled bear, which is also known as the Andean bear. It is the only bear native to South America and lives in the dense cloud forests of the Tropical Andes. An excellent climber, it eats and sleeps high in the trees. When ripe fruit is not available, these bears forage on the ground for plants and tree bark, but their home is disappearing fast due to agriculture, logging, and mining. The forest is vulnerable to the climate crisis, too. Sometimes bears are deliberately killed, either by farmers who are protecting their crops or cattle, or for the supposed medicinal benefits of their claws and other body parts.

Many international organizations are working together to develop a conservation strategy across the region. One of their priorities is to find solutions to conflicts between wild bears and farmers, developing a communication campaign and identifying priority sites for bear conservation. So far, a total of 58 protected areas have been established across the Andean bear distribution.

| Population trend | **Increasing** |
| --- | --- |
| Habitats | **Wetlands, marine coastal** |
| Distribution | **Canada, United States** |
| Threats | **Poaching, habitat loss, predation, disturbance** |

EX  EW  CR  **EN**  VU  NT  LC
▲

# Whooping crane

*Grus americana*

At five feet (one-and-a-half meters) tall, the whooping crane is the tallest bird in North America and is known for its loud, clear call. On stretches of wetland and coastal marshes, it forages for crustaceans, small fish, and amphibians, and grazes on grains and marsh plants. Each whooping crane is monogamous and will mate for life. When an infant crane hatches, it will imprint on the first moving creature it sees, recognising that creature as its parent for as long as it lives. Once found across much of North America, the crane is now endangered due to hunting and its wetland habitats being drained and replaced by farmland. The only naturally occurring flock of wild migratory whooping cranes left in the world is one that migrates every spring between a wildlife refuge in Texas to a national park in Canada.

The Whooping Crane Recovery Team has established an intensive conservation plan to save these cranes from extinction. This includes habitat management, together with captive breeding and reintroduction programs.

| | |
|---:|:---|
| Population trend | **Decreasing** |
| Habitats | **Marine** |
| Distribution | **Pacific and Indian Oceans** |
| Threats | **Overfishing, bycatch, wildlife trade** |

EX EW CR EN **VU** NT LC
▲

# Hedgehog seahorse
*Hippocampus spinosissimus*

With a horse-like head, monkey tail, kangaroo pouch, and eyes that can swivel independently of each other, the seahorse is a remarkable fish. Instead of scales, it has thin skin stretched over a series of bony plates. One of over 40 different species, the hedgehog seahorse is distinguished by its coronet and spiny body. Found in temperate and shallow coastal waters, it feeds on small crustaceans and shrimps on soft sand and silt. Hedgehog seahorses are declining across their range. In the Philippines, Malaysia, and Thailand over the past decade the hedgehog seahorse's population may have decreased by 30 percent or more. They are one of the most traded seahorses, for both traditional medicine and the aquarium trade.

Project Seahorse collaborates with researchers and global institutions to develop research to drive the recovery of seahorse populations and habitats. It has generated dozens of locally managed, marine-protected areas and trained over 175 professional conservationists and many citizen scientists.

| | |
|---:|:---|
| Population trend | **Decreasing** |
| Habitats | **Forest** |
| Distribution | **Sri Lanka** |
| Threats | **Habitat loss, deforestation, conflict** |

EX EW CR **EN** VU NT LC
▲

# Purple-faced langur
*Trachypithecus vetulus*

The purple-faced langur, also known as the purple-faced leaf monkey, is found only in the tropical rainforest of Sri Lanka. This very shy species lives in the tree canopy and prefers to eat young leaves rich in protein. The langurs once lived all over the island, but 90 percent of their rainforest has gone, forcing them to live alongside humans, in gardens and on rooftops, feeding on cultivated fruits, rather than leaves. Increasing clashes between humans and monkeys have caused these langurs to be labelled as pests who raid kitchens and damage roofs. Langurs are killed as they try to cross roads or when they touch overhead electrical cables.

The Sri Lanka Department of Forest Conservation is educating the public on the many endangered species on the island, including the purple-faced langur. Rope bridges have been installed to try to avoid langurs being killed on roads.

| | |
|---|---|
| Population trend | **Decreasing** |
| Habitats | **Grassland** |
| Distribution | **South Africa** |
| Threats | **Habitat loss and fragmentation, wildlife trade** |

EX EW CR EN **VU** NT LC

# Giant dragon lizard

*Smaug giganteus*

Giant dragon lizards, also known as sungazer lizards, are only found in the Highveld grasslands of South Africa. They are named after their habit of appearing to look into the sun as they bask. Resembling a miniature dragon, this species is the inspiration behind the fantastical character Smaug in J.R.R. Tolkein's *The Hobbit*. The sharp, bony spikes that cover its body protect the lizard from predators such as jackals and birds of prey. Unfortunately, they offer little protection from the humans ploughing up large tracts of habitat for agriculture, which is leaving populations fragmented and isolated. Sungazers are also taken from the wild for the illegal pet trade. They have declined by more than a third over the past 10 years.

The Sungazer Conservation Project is working with farmers and building relationships with landowners who have sungazer populations on their estates. Their aim is to protect more habitats and to raise public awareness concerning the impacts of keeping reptiles in captivity.

| | |
|---|---|
| Population trend | **Unknown** |
| Habitats | **Wetlands** |
| Distribution | **Caspian Sea** |
| Threats | **Bycatch, hunting, disease** |

EX EW CR **EN** VU NT LC

# Caspian seal

*Pusa caspica*

The Caspian seal is the only marine mammal in the Caspian Sea, landlocked by Russia, Azerbaijan, Iran, Turkmenistan, and Kazakhstan. It is a key indicator for the health of the Caspian Sea, which thousands of people depend on for their livelihoods. It is found along the shoreline and on the many rocky islands and floating blocks of ice. At the start of the 20th century there were around one million Caspian seals. Since then, the population has decreased by more than 90 percent. This decline is directly related to intensive hunting, which has been ongoing since the mid-18th century, with tens of thousands of seals killed at their breeding grounds on the winter ice fields every year. Seals are also caught annually in large mesh nets, which have been illegally set for sturgeon.

The first and foremost goal of the Caspian Seal Project, an initiative involving scientists from each of the five countries surrounding the Caspian Sea, is to stop all deliberate killing of Caspian seals.

| | |
|---:|:---|
| Population trend | **Decreasing** |
| Habitats | **Forest, savanna, shrubland** |
| Distribution | **Ethiopia, Kenya, Somalia** |
| Threats | **Poaching, hunting, habitat loss, agriculture, drought, conflict** |

EX  EW  CR  **EN**  VU  NT  LC

# Reticulated giraffe

*Giraffa camelopardalis reticulata*

The reticulated or Somali giraffe is the most well known of the nine giraffe subspecies, easily identified by a pattern of large, russet-colored blocks outlined by bright white lines. The giraffe's extraordinary height enables it to feed on the leaves, twigs, and bark of acacia trees, which other animals are unable to reach. Although they are fast runners and can gallop up to 35 miles per hour, they are relatively easy targets for humans with guns and traps. Poachers use the giraffe's tail and skin to make bracelets and shoelaces, and the meat can feed a village, which means their numbers continue to decrease. Reticulated giraffes are now classified as Endangered, with only around 9,000 animals remaining across the open forests, dry savannas, rainforests, and plains of Kenya, Ethiopia, and Somalia. Habitat loss is also having a negative impact.

The Giraffe Conservation Foundation is one of several organizations developing collaborative approaches with local people to halt the decline.

| | |
|---:|:---|
| Population trend | **Decreasing** |
| Habitats | **Forest** |
| Distribution | **Sri Lanka** |
| Threats | **Habitat loss, wildlife trade, hunting** |

EX　EW　CR　**EN**　VU　NT　LC
▲

# Red slender loris

*Loris tardigradus*

The red slender loris is a small nocturnal primate, living in the lowland rainforests of Sri Lanka. With enormous forward-facing eyes and long, thin limbs, it has excellent night vision and is a highly skilled climber, able to bridge large gaps between trees. It is among the most social of the nocturnal primates and mainly feeds on insects – although birds' eggs, geckos, and lizards are also eaten, including the scales and bones. Red slender lorises experience the same pressures as their Javan cousins, the slow lorises: their numbers are decreasing as their forest homes are destroyed, and those still living there are often captured and sold as pets. Some local people believe the lorises have magical medicinal powers, so they are also captured and killed for their body parts.

International researchers are gathering data on loris distribution, habitat preferences, and threats. Restoration work is underway to repair and connect fragmented forest patches containing their populations.

| | |
|---|---|
| Population trend | **Unknown** |
| Habitats | **Forest, shrubland** |
| Distribution | **Galápagos Islands (Ecuador)** |
| Threats | **Hunting, habitat loss, invasive species** |

EX  EW  CR  **EN**  VU  NT  LC
▲

# Volcán Darwin giant tortoise

*Chelonoidis microphyes* and other related species

This giant tortoise is found only on a chain of volcanic islands off the coast of Ecuador in South America. It is the largest tortoise in the world and can live to 100 years old. There are many subspecies of giant tortoises living on different islands. Some have saddleback shells that rise at the front, making it easier for them to lift their heads high to feed; others have dome-shaped shells, and live where vegetation is closer to the ground. Two centuries ago, these islands were home to more than 200,000 giant tortoises. Today, four species are extinct and only about 20,000 tortoises remain. Galápagos tortoises are threatened by invasive species such as cats and dogs, habitat destruction, and increasing human-tortoise conflicts.

The aim of the Giant Tortoise Restoration Initiative is to restore tortoise populations to their historical distribution and number throughout the whole archipelago.

| | |
|---|---|
| Population trend | **Decreasing** |
| Habitats | **Forest, shrubland** |
| Distribution | **Bhutan, China, Nepal** |
| Threats | **Habitat loss** |

EX EW CR **EN** VU NT LC
▲

# Red panda
*Ailurus fulgens*

Red pandas are shy, solitary animals, spending most of their lives in trees. With semi-retractable claws and an extended wrist bone that acts as a thumb, red pandas are expert climbers, moving easily from branch to branch. They use their long, bushy tails for balance and to cover themselves in winter to keep warm. They mainly feed on bamboo, although they will also eat insects, fruit, roots, and eggs. They are most active at dawn, dusk, and during the night. The loss of nesting trees and bamboo across China and the eastern Himalayas has left the red panda endangered. They are now protected, meaning that hunting them is illegal, but more work is needed to make sure they don't disappear altogether.

International organizations are working with local communities to reduce human impact on the red pandas' habitat. This includes monitoring populations and working with yak herders and community groups.

| | |
|---:|:---|
| Population trend | **Decreasing** |
| Habitats | **Savanna, shrubland, grassland, desert** |
| Distribution | **Africa** |
| Threats | **Habitat loss, wildlife trade, conflict** |

EX EW CR EN VU NT LC
▲

# Cheetah

*Acinonyx jubatus*

Built for speed, the cheetah is a slender cat with long limbs and a muscular tail, which is used for balance and steering. It is the fastest land animal in the world, reaching speeds of up to 64 miles per hour to intercept prey in the open grasslands of Africa. Cheetahs are the only big cats that can turn in mid-air while sprinting. They are also Africa's most threatened large cat, with fewer than 7,000 remaining. Historically, they have been hunted for their fur, but today the biggest threats cheetahs face are habitat loss and competition for resources. Increased human settlements, agriculture, and road construction are reducing their habitats. As their natural prey declines, cheetahs may attack livestock, leading them into conflict with farmers.

Conservationists are working to change local people's attitudes and provide better ways to guard their livestock. Nearly every African range state is involved with the Range Wide Conservation Program for Cheetah and African Wild Dogs (RWCP), which supports them in the development of regional strategies and national conservation action plans.

| | |
|---|---|
| Population trend | **Decreasing** |
| Habitats | **Forest, shrubland, grassland** |
| Distribution | **Central, South, and Southeast Asia** |
| Threats | **Habitat loss, hunting, persecution, disease** |

EX  EW  CR  **EN**  VU  NT  LC

# Dhole
*Cuon alpinus*

The dhole, or Asian wild dog, wanders through dense forest, often at high altitude. It has an eerie, whistling call, which it uses to gather pack members together. This has given rise to its other common name, the whistling dog. Dholes are fast runners, excellent swimmers, and impressive jumpers – all useful hunting skills that also come in handy when avoiding resident tigers and leopards. In the past 50 years, their numbers have plummeted across Asia, most likely because of loss of habitat and a decline in the species they feed on. Palm oil, paper, rubber, and timber production, as well as mining, has led to the destruction of much of their forest home, and the small amount of forest that remains has become fragmented by growing human populations, roads, and development.

By tracking animals with satellite collars, monitoring human-dhole conflict, and carrying out community outreach, conservationists are trying to prevent this animal from becoming extinct.

| | |
|---|---|
| Population trend | **Decreasing** |
| Habitats | **Forest, shrubland, grassland** |
| Distribution | **India, Southeast Asia** |
| Threats | **Habitat loss, agriculture, conflict, poaching, wildlife trade** |

EX EW CR **EN** VU NT LC

# Asian elephant
*Elephas maximus*

Asian elephants live in lush, wet, humid tropical forests. They are the ecosystem engineers of their habitat, clearing large areas of vegetation and creating space for new growth. They tend to be smaller than African elephants and have smaller, more-rounded ears. The Asian elephant also has a twin-domed head and a long, tapered lower lip. Only some of the male Asian elephants have tusks. Over the past 75 years it is estimated that the population of Asian elephants has declined by 50 percent. Almost a third of Asian elephants live in captivity, increasingly used in the tourism industry. Those that live in the wild are coming into ever more conflict with local communities in food-producing areas.

Conservationists are working with local communities to reduce human-elephant conflict, protect elephant habitat, and restore wildlife corridors. They are also trying to stop poaching for the wildlife trade.

| | |
|---:|:---|
| Population trend | **Decreasing** |
| Habitats | **Forest** |
| Distribution | **Europe** |
| Threats | **Habitat loss** |

EX EW CR EN VU **NT** LC
▲

# Stag beetle
*Lucanus cervus*

Stag beetles are large land beetles that live in woodland, hedgerows, parks, and gardens. Adult males can grow to three inches (75 millimeters) in length and have characteristic "antlers," which are actually huge jaws designed for wrestling rivals. Common names include "thunder beetle" and "horse pincher." Despite their fearsome appearance and nicknames, they are completely harmless to humans. They have a fascinating life cycle, feeding on dead wood for up to seven years until they are ready to emerge as adults, leaving behind a distinctive network of tunnels. As a result of their long development, stag beetles are vulnerable to predators, particularly magpies, and suffer enormously from habitat destruction. These amazing creatures used to be a common sight, especially in the south of England, but they are now declining throughout their European range.

Stag beetles are protected in the UK and a priority species for conservation action. Conservationists are carrying out annual surveys and encouraging people to leave dead trees and stumps, or to build log piles in their gardens.

| Population trend | **Decreasing** |
| --- | --- |
| Habitats | **Forest, grassland** |
| Distribution | **Canada, United States** |
| Threats | **Habitat loss, disease, pesticides, climate change** |

EX EW **CR** EN VU NT LC
▲

# Rusty patched bumblebee

*Bombus affinis*

The rusty patched bumblebee gets its name because of the small rust-colored patch on its back. It is an important pollinator of crops, such as blueberries, cranberries, and tomatoes. Once a common sight in hedgerows, parks, and gardens across huge swathes of North America, the bee's population has plummeted by nearly 90 percent since the 1990s. Intensive use of agricultural land and the conversion of grassland to monoculture landscapes have resulted in the destruction of bumblebee nesting and overwintering sites, as well as disturbance of foraging grounds. The unpredictability of a changing climate, including warmer periods, early snow, late frost, and drought, also has an impact.

The rusty patched bumblebee is the first bee species in the continental United States to join the endangered species list. Conservationists are working on three key areas to keep this species from becoming extinct: reducing pesticide use, creating wildflower habitats, and ensuring there are safe places for bees to build their underground nests for the winter.

| | |
|---:|:---|
| Population trend | **Decreasing** |
| Habitats | **Forest, grassland, wetlands** |
| Distribution | **Malaysia, Myanmar, Sumatra (Indonesia), Thailand** |
| Threats | **Habitat loss, hunting, roadkill, fire** |

# Malayan tapir

*Tapirus indicus*

A relative of the horse and the rhino, the Malayan tapir is the heftiest of the tapir species. One local name for them is *badak tampung*, meaning "patched rhino." It has a well-armoured neck with skin up to an inch (three centimeters) thick, to protect it from tigers and other predators. It is shy, mainly active at night, and uses its prehensile upper lip to graze on foliage, fruit, and aquatic plants. All tapirs are strong swimmers and spend much of their time submerged, using their trunk-like nose as a snorkel. Malayan tapir numbers have dropped by more than 50 percent in the past 36 years, as the animal's habitat has been converted to oil palm plantations and housing. They are also threatened by hunting, poaching, and road traffic.

International initiatives are underway to protect this tapir, focusing efforts on protecting where it lives. The species is now legally protected in all range states, and large parts of its habitat are protected, including several national parks in Thailand, Myanmar, Peninsula Malaysia, and Sumatra.

| | |
|---:|:---|
| Population trend | **Stable** |
| Habitats | **Wetlands** |
| Distribution | **Argentina, Bolivia, Chile, Peru** |
| Threats | **Habitat loss, mining, poaching, disturbance** |

EX EW CR EN VU NT LC

# Andean flamingo

*Phoenicoparrus andinus*

The Andean flamingo is one of the rarest flamingos in the world and the only flamingo to have yellow legs and feet. It lives in highland salt lakes in the Andes Mountains. They travel vast distances between lagoons and ponds in search of food, usually at night and in a huge flock. One of the ways they communicate with one another is the wing salute, where they spread their wings out to show off their colors. They are filter feeders, which means they stir up water with their feet, submerge their head and beak, then suck up water and mud to extract plankton, insect larvae, and small fish. Mining activities near nesting sites, egg collecting, poaching, and uncontrolled ecotourism have all had a negative impact on these wading birds.

The populations of Andean flamingos are monitored through surveys. Outreach programs are being implemented in the most sensitive regions, and conservation work includes habitat management and prevention of egg collecting.

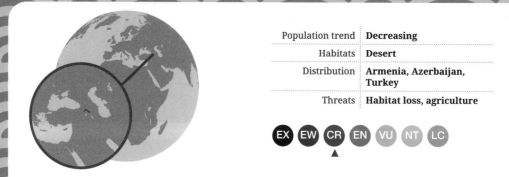

| Population trend | **Decreasing** |
|---|---|
| Habitats | **Desert** |
| Distribution | **Armenia, Azerbaijan, Turkey** |
| Threats | **Habitat loss, agriculture** |

EX EW **CR** EN VU NT LC
▲

# Horvath's toad-headed agama

*Phrynocephalus horvathi*

This small, critically endangered lizard is more commonly known as the Persian toad-headed agama. It has cryptic coloring and scales of different sizes and shapes, enabling it to become almost invisible in a landscape of bare rock and sand. To make the most of rare rainfall, it has evolved networks of "drinking straws" between its scales to suck up water through its skin. It also cleverly aligns its body, flattening its back to create a slope, to direct the flow of water to the tip of its snout. As the human population increases and land is built on or used for agriculture, the habitat of these lizards is becoming fragmented or lost entirely. Eighty percent of its habitat has been lost over the past 12 years.

Conservation groups are working urgently to identify remaining populations of these lizards.

| | |
|---:|:---|
| Population trend | **Decreasing** |
| Habitats | **Marine** |
| Distribution | **Atlantic, Pacific, and Indian Oceans** |
| Threats | **Poaching of eggs, wildlife trade, bycatch, pollution** |

EX · EW · **CR** · EN · VU · NT · LC
▲

# Hawksbill turtle

*Eretmochelys imbricata*

The hawksbill is named for its narrow head and beak-like jaw. It is the only turtle with a distinctive pattern of overlapping scales on its shell. With a small, agile body it can forage in shallow lagoons and coastal reefs that other species cannot reach. Hawksbill turtles also keep coral reefs healthy. They mainly feed on sponges, which they prise from crevices in the reefs, providing better access for fish to feed. Despite being protected, these creatures are hunted for their shells, known as tortoiseshell, which is used to make jewelry and ornaments. They also become tangled in fishing nets and drown, their eggs are harvested for food, and they can die as a consequence of eating plastic bags, which they mistake for jellyfish.

Marine conservationists are helping to strengthen protection laws for sea turtles. They are working with governments and local communities to make sure that local fishermen are managing their catches within the law. An increased interest in ecotourism is also helping the turtles.

| | |
|---|---|
| Population trend | **Unknown** |
| Habitats | **Forest, shrubland, grassland, marine** |
| Distribution | **Arctic Circle** |
| Threats | **Climate change, oil exploration, pollution, conflict** |

EX EW CR EN **VU** NT LC
▲

# Polar bear
*Ursus maritimus*

Mighty polar bears are the only bear species to be considered marine mammals because they spend most of their lives on the sea ice of the Arctic Ocean. Their Latin name means "sea bear." They use their strong sense of smell to hunt for ringed and bearded seals, which they can detect from up to two-thirds of a mile away. They also scavenge for whale and walrus carcasses. They are excellent long-distance swimmers and can swim for days to reach the next piece of ice, to hunt, or to find a mate.

Rising temperatures as a result of the climate crisis are the biggest threat to polar bears, drastically shrinking the sea ice and restricting their feeding range. The sea ice is important to polar bears' main prey of seals, as the seals make dens on the ice to give birth to pups. The Arctic is also potentially at risk from habitat destruction from oil exploration work. Our use of fossil fuels directly impacts the Arctic ecosystem, which supports polar bears and other wildlife, so we are all responsible for reducing the amount we use.

| | |
|---:|:---|
| Population trend | **Decreasing** |
| Habitats | **Savanna, grassland** |
| Distribution | **Bolivia, Brazil, Paraguay** |
| Threats | **Habitat loss, agriculture** |

(EX) (EW) (CR) (EN) (VU) (NT) (LC)
▲

# White-winged nightjar

*Eleothreptus candicans*

During the day this rare South American nightjar rests, hidden in dense vegetation. Thanks to its camouflage, it is difficult to spot. At dusk, it hunts for flying insects in forest clearings with scattered trees, anthills, and termite mounds. In flight, the white markings on the male's outer-wing feathers and the white tail can be seen. This species is threatened by habitat loss, as its grassland habitats are being turned into industrial-scale agriculture, or destroyed by invasive grasses and grazing. It is believed that there are less than a few hundred birds in the wild.

The future of the white-winged nightjar depends on the conservation of what remains of Cerrado habitat (dry grassland). Originally, Cerrado was the second largest habitat type in South America. It has the highest biodiversity of any savanna ecosystem in the world. Today, less than 25 percent of its original area remains intact. The white-winged nightjar is protected under Paraguayan and Brazilian law.

| Population trend | **Decreasing** |
| --- | --- |
| Habitats | **Shrubland, grassland, rocky areas, desert** |
| Distribution | **Central Asia** |
| Threats | **Habitat loss, hunting** |

EX EW CR EN VU NT **LC**
▲

# Pallas's cat

*Otocolobus manul*

Pallas's cats spend most of their time hiding in rocky crevices across the Central Asian steppes. They have the longest and densest fur of the cat family, enabling them to crouch and hunt on frozen ground. The scientific name means "ugly-eared," a reference to the cat's unusually small ears, which sit flat against its head and help the cat to remain hidden from view. The greatest threats to Pallas's cats are loss of habitat and loss of their prey through farming, agricultural activities, mining, and poisoning of pika (a distant cousin of the rabbit). They are also killed in traps laid for wolves and foxes, or by domestic dogs. Despite international trading bans and legal protections in some countries, they are hunted for their fur.

The Pallas's Cat International Conservation Alliance (PICA) is carrying out research into the ecology and distribution of these cats so that targeted conservation plans can be put into practice.

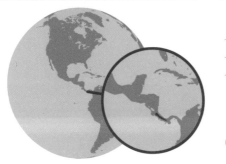

| | |
|---|---|
| Population trend | **Decreasing** |
| Habitats | **Forest, wetlands** |
| Distribution | **Costa Rica, Panama** |
| Threats | **Habitat loss, deforestation, disease, predation** |

EX  EW  CR  EN  VU  NT  LC

# Variable harlequin frog

*Atelopus varius*

Variable harlequin frogs, or clown frogs, are known for their bright colors, which serve as a warning to potential predators that they are poisonous. They normally live among fallen leaves on the rainforest floor. Their patterns vary hugely from population to population – even frogs that live close to each other can look completely different. Dramatic declines in variable harlequin frog populations began in the late 1980s, and they continue to fall. In the early 1990s these frogs disappeared suddenly from Costa Rica and Panama, and they now exist only in a handful of locations. Areas of rainforest where harlequins live are being cut down and a parasitic fungus that infects the skin of amphibians has affected this and many other frog species across the globe.

The species is present in three protected areas in Panama and a captive breeding program is underway. According to the IUCN Red List of Threatened Species, 41 percent of all the amphibian species known to science are currently threatened.

| | |
|---:|:---|
| Population trend | **Decreasing** |
| Habitats | **Forest** |
| Distribution | **Congo Basin (Africa)** |
| Threats | **Hunting, habitat loss, deforestation, conflict** |

EX  EW  CR  **EN**  VU  NT  LC
▲

# Bonobo
*Pan paniscus*

Also known as pygmy chimpanzees, bonobos live in the tropical forests of the central Congo Basin. Led by females, bonobo society follows a sophisticated structure that encourages cooperation and peace. Bonobos feed mainly in trees and descend to the ground to move to other trees. They eat mostly fruits, which they often share with one another, and other vegetation such as herbs and roots. The number of bonobos in the wild is shrinking because of human destruction of forests and illegal hunting of these apes for meat. It is estimated that there are only 30,000 bonobos remaining. Bonobos are protected by national and international laws throughout their range, and the majority are found in national parks.

To help protect them, conservationists are working with local people to monitor the area and use CyberTracker technology to collect data on where the animals are, and where there is evidence of human encroachment. This knowledge means they are better placed to target their resources in the areas where they will be most effective.

| | |
|---:|:---|
| Population trend | **Decreasing** |
| Habitats | **Forest, shrubland, grassland** |
| Distribution | **Central Europe** |
| Threats | **Habitat loss, agriculture** |

EX  EW  CR  EN  VU  NT  LC
▲

# Lulworth skipper
*Thymelicus acteon*

This small butterfly was first discovered in Lulworth Cove in Dorset, England, in 1832, hence its name. Lulworth skipper females have distinctive pale-orange "sun ray" markings on their forewings. The males are darker with almost olive-colored wings and a black line through the middle of the forewing. They can still be found in large numbers in the extreme south of Dorset, but Lulworth skippers are declining across Europe. They have very specific habitat requirements: adult females lay their eggs on tor-grass and previous surveys suggest that they like it to be long, so the species may lose out in areas grazed by livestock or rabbits.

The Lulworth skipper has the European status of Vulnerable and is a UK Biodiversity Action Plan Priority Species. Further surveying and monitoring is needed to assess the role of vegetation structure and the increasing pressures of a changing environment.

| | |
|---|---|
| Population trend | **Increasing** |
| Habitats | **Forest, savanna, shrubland, grassland, wetlands, desert** |
| Distribution | **Sub-Saharan Africa** |
| Threats | **Wildlife trade, hunting, habitat loss, conflict** |

EX  EW  CR  EN  VU  NT  LC
▲

# African elephant
*Loxodonta africana*

The African elephant is the world's largest land mammal, growing to between eight and 13 feet (two-and-a-half and four meters) tall. It is famous for its large ears, which help to keep it cool in a baking-hot climate. Both males and females grow ivory tusks, which are actually elongated incisors. In areas where they are protected, numbers are increasing. However, illegal poaching has been getting worse in some parts of Africa, mostly due to the demand for ivory in China and the Far East. It's estimated that 20,000 African elephants are killed every year for their ivory. This, together with habitat loss and conflict with people, means they continue to be at risk.

Organizations, such as the WWF, help governments to produce elephant conservation strategies, allowing them to monitor and manage populations and reduce the illegal trade in elephant products. Community-based conservation programs, including ones to divert the revenue from the sport of hunting elephants back to communities, are increasing tolerance of larger numbers of elephants.

| | |
|---:|:---|
| Population trend | **Decreasing** |
| Habitats | **Forest, wetlands** |
| Distribution | **South America** |
| Threats | **Hunting, habitat loss, overfishing, conflict, pollution, climate change** |

EX EW CR EN VU NT LC

# Giant otter

*Pteronura brasiliensis*

When fully grown, the giant otter is almost seven feet (two meters) long. It swims in the remote tropical rivers and creeks of the Amazon, Orinoco, and La Plata river systems and has earned itself the name of "river wolf." Most commonly preying on fish, it has been known to attack caiman and anacondas. With webbed feet, water-repellent fur, and nostrils and ears that close when they are in water, they are well adapted to aquatic life. They hunt with precision and speed, thanks to strong eyesight, powerful tails and streamlined bodies, and sometimes do so alone, but more often in groups.

Giant otters were almost wiped out due to demand for their fur. Following the banning of the fur trade, numbers started to recover, but there are now several emerging threats, including deforestation and gold mining, which pollutes the rivers. They also come into conflict with local fishermen. Conservationists are monitoring giant otter populations and engaging with local communities to reduce activities that are harmful to them. They are working with local government agencies to manage their habitat.

| | |
|---|---|
| Population trend | **Unspecified** |
| Habitats | **Savanna, grassland** |
| Distribution | **United States** |
| Threats | **Unknown** |

EX EW **CR** EN VU NT LC

# American burying beetle

*Nicrophorus americanus*

Growing to up to one-and-a-half inches (four centimeters) long, American burying beetles are the largest of the carrion beetles. These shiny, black beetles have orange bands on their wing covers and a distinctive orange marking just behind the head. They are nocturnal and one of nature's most efficient recyclers, burying dead animals to feed on and returning valuable nutrients to the soil. Insects, mice, birds, and snakes all form part of their diet. Burying beetles are unusual in that both the male and female take part in raising their young. Since the early 1900s they have been disappearing from across the United States. It is thought habitat loss, scarcity of carcasses, use of pesticides, and increased light pollution are the main causes.

Conservationists continue to work on reintroduction programs in Massachusetts, Ohio, and Missouri. In Rhode Island, schoolchildren campaigned for the beetle to be given the title of state insect, as a way to raise public awareness of its plight. In 2015, the American burying beetle was designated the official state insect of Rhode Island.

| | |
|---|---|
| Population trend | **Decreasing** |
| Habitats | **Forest, shrubland, grassland, rocky areas** |
| Distribution | **Central Asia** |
| Threats | **Habitat loss, poaching, decline in prey** |

EX EW CR EN **VU** NT LC
▲

# Snow leopard

*Panthera uncia*

The handsome snow leopard is specially adapted for living in a cold, mountainous environment. Its small, rounded ears help to minimize heat loss, and enormous paws with furry undersides are perfect for walking on snow and rugged ground. Its noticeably long, thick tail is not only useful for balance, but also to wrap it around its body and face when asleep. As one of the top predators in the high-mountain food web, the snow leopard helps to keep the alpine meadows healthy by preying on marmots, ibexes, and other native herbivores. However, numbers have declined by 20 percent in the past 20 years due to poaching and habitat loss. It is estimated that there are between 3,920 and 6,390 snow leopards left in the wild, with China and Mongolia home to the majority.

Various international and national laws protect the snow leopard. A number of governments have also created national parks to preserve their habitat.

| | |
|---:|:---|
| Population trend | **Decreasing** |
| Habitats | **Forest, shrubland** |
| Distribution | **Southeast Asia** |
| Threats | **Habitat loss, hunting, wildlife trade** |

EX EW CR EN **VU** NT LC

# Sun bear

*Helarctos malayanus*

The sun bear is the smallest member of the bear family and lives a reclusive life in the remote tropical forests of Southeast Asia. Despite their name, sun bears are active at night, foraging for fruit, roots, and small animals. Legend has it that the golden patch on their chest represents the rising sun. Their velvety coat is short enough to avoid overheating in the tropical climate, but thick enough to provide protection from twigs, branches, and rain. It is estimated that there has been a loss of more than 30 percent of these bears in the past 30 years. They are threatened by habitat loss due to deforestation, and hunting. Females are sometimes killed so that their cubs can be taken and sold as pets.

One of the main priorities for local communities, government organizations, and conservation charities is to protect the forest from further logging and plantations. They are also working to stop the rise in wildlife trade.

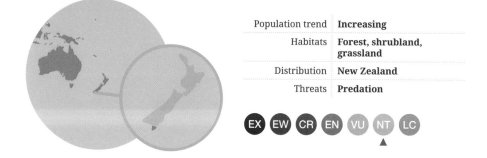

| | |
|---|---|
| Population trend | **Increasing** |
| Habitats | **Forest, shrubland, grassland** |
| Distribution | **New Zealand** |
| Threats | **Predation** |

EX EW CR EN VU **NT** LC

# Little spotted kiwi

*Apteryx owenii*

The adventurous little spotted kiwi is the smallest of the five kiwi species and is about the size of a bantam hen. It is flightless and nocturnal. It has a mottled grey, shaggy plumage and is the only bird that has nostrils on the tip of its beak. During the day, it rests in a hollow log, or burrow, and then emerges shortly after nightfall. It mainly feeds on earthworms and beetle larvae, which it detects by walking slowly, while tapping the ground. Little spotted kiwis are monogamous and generally mate for life. These birds are fiercely territorial and use their sharp claws to fight.

Kiwi numbers were devastated on the mainland by stoats, dogs, and cats. Without the sanctuary of predator-free offshore islands, the little spotted kiwi may have gone extinct. The population stronghold of an estimated 1,200 birds is on Kapiti Island. The number of little spotted kiwi is increasing as they are moved to more sites.

| | |
|---:|:---|
| Population trend | **Decreasing** |
| Habitats | **Forest, wetlands** |
| Distribution | **Asia, Europe** |
| Threats | **Habitat loss and fragmentation, pollution** |

EX  EW  CR  EN  VU  NT  **LC**
▲

# Great crested newt

*Triturus cristatus*

Resembling a miniature dragon, this amphibian can be identified by the pattern of black spots on their orange bellies, which is as unique as a fingerprint. Great crested newts breed in ponds in the spring, but for most of the year they can be found feeding on invertebrates in woodland, hedgerows, marshes, and grassland. In winter, they hibernate underground. It is the male newt that has the distinctive wavy crest that runs along its back. The loss of ponds is the biggest threat to these newts, together with the fragmentation of habitat on land.

The UK populations of this newt are internationally important, so much so that they are protected under both British and European law. Across Britain, conservationists are working with farmers, landowners, and planners to ensure they are protected.

| | |
|---|---|
| Population trend | **Decreasing** |
| Habitats | **Shrubland, grassland, wetlands** |
| Distribution | **Central Asia, Eastern Europe, North Africa** |
| Threats | **Habitat loss, wildlife trade** |

EX  EW  CR  **EN**  VU  NT  LC

# Saker falcon

*Falco cherrug*

This large falcon is found in open grasslands with rocky areas and cliffs. It hunts by horizontal pursuit and feeds mainly on rodents and birds. Like most falcons, they don't build nests but reuse the nests of other large birds. Saker falcon populations have declined rapidly – by as much as 90 percent – and it has become one of the most endangered falcons in the world. This has been caused by intensive agriculture leading to critical habitat loss, pesticide use, persecution, and electrocution on power lines, as well as nest robbery. Falcons are illegally captured and sold for large sums of money on the black market. In 2012, it was estimated that the population size was between 12,200 and 29,800.

The saker falcon is recognized under all major conventions as being a globally threatened species of special conservation concern. Several charities are working to prevent the extinction of this magnificent bird, focusing efforts in Bulgaria. Conservation work includes installing artificial nests and DNA profiling.

| | |
|---:|:---|
| Population trend | **Decreasing** |
| Habitats | **Forest** |
| Distribution | **Southeast Madagascar** |
| Threats | **Deforestation, mining** |

# Anosy mouse lemur

*Microcebus tanosi*

The Anosy mouse lemur was discovered as recently as 2007 and has been classified as Endangered, due to the dramatic loss of its habitat in the Sainte Luce Littoral Forest. Compared to other mouse lemurs, it is large, measuring about 11 inches (27 centimeters) long. It is nocturnal and omnivorous, remaining solitary or keeping to small groups. Like its neighbors, the Anosy mouse lemur is suffering from the destruction of its home through deforestation.

The team at SEED Madagascar are monitoring the lemurs' movements and behaviors. This will help them evaluate how effective forest corridors are as a conservation strategy. Together with its partners, it is trying to regenerate the forest and support sustainable, community-led natural resource management, meaning a better future for people, lemurs, and other animals that depend on the forest.

| Population trend | **Decreasing** |
| --- | --- |
| Habitats | **River** |
| Distribution | **Yangtze River (China)** |
| Threats | **Hunting, bycatch, pollution** |

(EX) (EW) **(CR)** (EN) (VU) (NT) (LC)

# Baiji

*Lipotes vexillifer*

Although it is listed as Critically Endangered on the IUCN's Red List, there have been no sightings of baiji, also called Chinese river dolphins, since 2006. This means that it is probably the first species of dolphin to become extinct due to the impact of humans. For 20 million years this freshwater dolphin, known as the "goddess of the Yangtze," lived along Asia's longest river. Quiet and shy, with very poor eyesight, they had a highly developed and sensitive sonar system. As the Yangtze River became increasingly busy with thousands of noisy ships, these dolphins could no longer communicate, navigate, avoid danger, or find food by using echolocation. The situation became even worse with the construction of the Three-Gorges Dam, causing wide-scale environmental damage to the Yangtze River and destroying wildlife habitats.

It is a stark reminder of what can happen to our wildlife and why we must do all we can to stop more extinctions.

| | |
|---:|:---|
| Population trend | **Decreasing** |
| Habitats | **Forest** |
| Distribution | **Europe, Northern Asia** |
| Threats | **Competition, disease, habitat loss** |

EX EW CR EN VU NT **LC**
▲

# Eurasian red squirrel

*Sciurus vulgaris*

The Eurasian red squirrel has distinctive, fiery-colored fur, prominent tufts above its ears, and a large bushy tail, which is almost as long as its body. It lives in coniferous, broadleaved, and mixed woodland and travels through the tree canopy with great agility. Pine seeds are a favourite food, together with hazelnuts, green acorns, and the seeds of larch and spruce. Once common across the UK, red squirrels have now disappeared from most of England and Wales. The largest populations can be found in the Highlands, in remnants of Caledonian Forest. They are faced with habitat fragmentation and competition from larger gray squirrels, a non-native squirrel introduced from North America in the 19th century. It is also susceptible to the spread of squirrel pox.

Red Squirrels United, a partnership of academics, conservationists, and volunteers, was launched in 2015 and together they are delivering a program of red squirrel conservation and control of the gray squirrel.

| | |
|---|---|
| Population trend | **Decreasing** |
| Habitats | **Marine** |
| Distribution | **Galápagos Islands (Ecuador)** |
| Threats | **Bycatch, climate change, land-based predators** |

EX  EW  CR  **EN**  VU  NT  LC
▲

# Galápagos penguin

*Spheniscus mendiculus*

This is the only penguin species found north of the equator and is one of the smallest and most endangered penguins in the world. Galápagos penguins are able to survive in the warm climate due to the cool, nutrient-rich waters of the Cromwell and Humboldt currents. They mainly feed on cold-water schooling fish, such as anchovies, sardines, and mullet. On land, Galápagos penguins live in caves and the crevices formed in coastal lava. Their breeding success is closely linked to environmental conditions, and the climate crisis is a major threat to their future. In 1982, a strong El Niño event caused 77 percent of the population to die of starvation because it reduced the strength of the cool currents, which these birds are reliant on as they bring nutrients to the surface of the water. In 2019, the population was estimated to be just 1,200 birds.

Conservationists have built 120 shaded nest sites constructed of stacked lava rocks and continue to monitor the population several times each year. More research is needed to prevent these penguins from becoming extinct.

| | |
|---|---|
| Population trend | **Decreasing** |
| Habitats | **Forest, savanna, shrubland, grassland, wetlands** |
| Distribution | **Central and South America, Mexico** |
| Threats | **Habitat loss, hunting, conflict, poaching** |

EX  EW  CR  EN  VU  NT  LC
▲

# Jaguar
*Panthera onca*

The muscular jaguar is the largest cat in the Americas, and the majority live in the rainforests and tropical wetlands of Central and South America. Although similar in appearance to the leopard, it has a broader head, stockier body, and more powerful jaws. Its coat features a rosette pattern, which is made up of a circle of spots encircling smaller spots. The jaguar is a skilful tree climber and will often pounce on unsuspecting prey below. Its name comes from the Native American word *yaguar*, meaning "he who kills with one leap." Jaguar numbers are falling because of deforestation, both for logging and to clear space for cattle ranching. Less habitat means jaguars' prey is reduced, which leads them to hunt livestock and be killed by people. Although hunting jaguars is illegal, they are also vulnerable to poaching.

Conservationists are working with governments, businesses, and landowners to map and protect jaguar populations and create wildlife corridors that cover 18 countries and two continents.

| | |
|---:|:---|
| Population trend | **Decreasing** |
| Habitats | **Grassland, desert** |
| Distribution | **Central Asia** |
| Threats | **Poaching, wildlife trade, habitat loss, disease** |

EX EW **CR** EN VU NT LC
▲

# Saiga
*Saiga tatarica*

The saiga antelope is ideally suited to the harsh conditions of semi-desert grassland along the Eurasian steppes. It has a dense fur coat and a bulbous nose with an unusual structure, which is thought to filter out dust in summer and warm the cold air in winter. Only males have the heavily ridged horns. Uncontrolled, illegal hunting for both their horns and meat has led to a catastrophic decline in saiga numbers. It has an estimated global population of 100,000, down from 1,250,000 in the mid 1970s. Increasingly, the fast pace of development of infrastructure for oil and gas extraction in Mongolia, Uzbekistan, and Kazakhstan is threatening the saigas' habitat.

Since 2006, the Saiga Conservation Alliance, a network of researchers and conservationists, have been working to save this rare animal. They are conducting fieldwork, education, and outreach to prevent it from being lost. Saiga Day is now celebrated every year in early May to mark the arrival of the first saiga calves, and helps to unite communities across the saiga's range states.

| | |
|---:|:---|
| Population trend | **Decreasing** |
| Habitats | **Forest, savanna, shrubland, grassland** |
| Distribution | **India, Nepal, Sri Lanka** |
| Threats | **Habitat loss, hunting** |

EX EW CR EN VU NT LC
▲

# Sloth bear

*Melursus ursinus*

With its unruly black fur and long, pale muzzle, this bear is unmistakable. Like the sloth, it also has impressive hooked claws, a shaggy coat, and no upper middle teeth. But, unlike the sloth, it is always busy, wandering through tropical forests in search of termite mounds and anthills. When it finds them, it rips them open with its claws and noisily vacuums up the insects through the gaps in its front teeth. It is also very fond of honey, hence the alternative name of honey bear. Sloth bears are threatened by habitat loss as their forest home is turned into agricultural land. They are also hunted for food, for their gallbladders, which are used in medicine, and because of their aggressive behavior and destruction of crops.

To halt the decline in bear numbers, national reforestation programs, coupled with local education initiatives, are needed to reduce conflicts between people and bears. Historically, sloth bears were captured to perform as dancing bears, but since 2012, this has stopped.

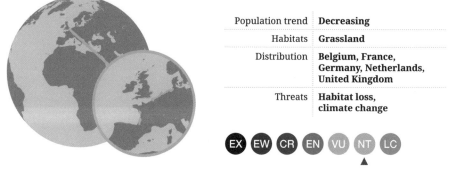

| | |
|---|---|
| Population trend | **Decreasing** |
| Habitats | **Grassland** |
| Distribution | **Belgium, France, Germany, Netherlands, United Kingdom** |
| Threats | **Habitat loss, climate change** |

EX EW CR EN VU **NT** LC
▲

# Sea aster mining bee

*Colletes halophilus*

Sea aster mining bees tend to be found along the sandy margins of saltmarshes from southern France to northwestern Germany, and along parts of southern and southeastern England, particularly in East Anglia and the Thames Estuary. The scientific name *halophilus* means "salt loving." The bee's common name is a reference to its preferred food source, sea aster, which flowers at the same time as the bee's August emergence, when they collect pollen and nectar for their young. However, the climate crisis and a rising sea are causing their saltmarsh habitat to be lost, with further impact on the bee's Thames Estuary populations from development pressure.

The UK supports nationally important populations of this bee. The People's Trust for Endangered Species has funded research with Buglife to understand what the bees need to thrive. Simple actions to provide nesting habitat in coastal areas that have an abundance of sea aster may make a positive difference. New development projects in the Thames Estuary could include nesting areas for this and many other insect species.

| | |
|---|---|
| Population trend | **Decreasing** |
| Habitats | **Forest, savanna, rocky areas** |
| Distribution | **Eastern Australia** |
| Threats | **Habitat loss, bush fire, climate change, competition, predation** |

EX  EW  CR  EN  VU  NT  LC

# Brush-tailed rock wallaby

*Petrogale penicillata*

There are 15 species of rock wallaby and eight subspecies. The brush-tailed rock wallaby has a white cheek stripe and a black stripe running from its forehead to the back of its head. Using its distinctive bushy tail for balance and padded feet for grip, it leaps and bounds around rocky outcrops, escarpments, and cliffs. It is an expert climber, scaling tall trees and almost-vertical rocks. At dawn and dusk, it descends from caves and ledges to graze and eat the leaves and fruit of shrubs and trees. This wallaby is threatened by introduced foxes and competition with feral goats. Devastating bush fires have wiped out huge swathes of its habitat and food, exacerbated by extended drought and high temperatures due to the climate crisis.

Faced with the gargantuan task of saving many dozens of threatened species during bush fires, the New South Wales National Parks and Wildlife Service launched Operation Rock Wallaby in 2020, conducting airdrops of carrots and sweet potatoes.

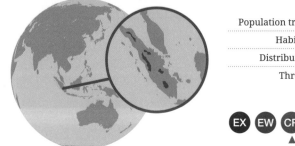

| | |
|---:|:---|
| Population trend | **Decreasing** |
| Habitats | **Forest** |
| Distribution | **Sumatra (Indonesia)** |
| Threats | **Habitat loss, poaching, wildlife trade** |

EX EW **CR** EN VU NT LC

# Sumatran tiger

*Panthera tigris sumatrae*

Sumatran tigers are only found on the Indonesian island of Sumatra, off the Malaysian Peninsula. Their habitat ranges from lowland forest to mountain forest. They are the smallest of the tiger species and have the narrowest black stripes, helping them to blend in with dense vegetation. Like all tigers, their pattern of stripes is unique to each individual. Although it is illegal to hunt Sumatran tigers, poaching of these animals for the illegal trading of their fur, bones, and body parts is a continuing threat. Sumatra has also seen a large-scale agricultural growth and this has fragmented the tigers' habitat. Consequently, Sumatran tigers are critically endangered, and conservationists estimate that there could be fewer than 400 of these tigers left in the wild.

A partnership of several international organizations is targeting four priority Tiger Conservation Landscapes in Sumatra to protect them through sustainable landscape management and to support the livelihoods of local communities living nearby.

| | |
|---:|:---|
| Population trend | **Unspecified** |
| Habitats | **Forest** |
| Distribution | **Africa, Asia, Europe** |
| Threats | **Habitat loss, wildlife trade** |

**EX** **EW** **CR** **EN** **VU** **NT** **LC**
▲

# Common tortoise

*Testudo graeca*

The common tortoise is also known as the Greek tortoise, since the pattern of flecks, lines, and spots on the shell are reminiscent of a Greek mosaic. Their color ranges from yellow-gold to dark brown or black. They are found from northern Morocco to southern Spain and Sicily. They prefer the semi-arid conditions of rocky hillsides, Mediterranean scrub, forests, and fields. They feed on a wide variety of woody plants, especially their flowers. From one to three raised scales, or spurs, are found on each thigh, either side of the tail. These tortoises are considered to be vulnerable because they are highly sought after by the illegal pet trade. As their habitat shrinks, there is less space for them to live in. They are an extremely long-living species and it isn't unusual for them to reach 125 years old.

Conservation work is taking place to release animals that have been confiscated from the illegal trade.

| Population trend | **Decreasing** |
| --- | --- |
| Habitats | **Forest** |
| Distribution | **Cameroon, Congo Basin, Nigeria** |
| Threats | **Hunting, wildlife trade, deforestation** |

EX  EW  **CR**  EN  VU  NT  LC

# Cross River gorilla

*Gorilla gorilla diehli*

Cross River gorillas, a subspecies of the western gorilla, are the most endangered of the African apes. They live in the rugged, mountainous border between Cameroon and Nigeria, at the top of the Cross River. Like all gorillas, they love fruits and will travel great distances to find their favorite, which is wild cardamom, a type of ginger plant. This region is populated by many humans, who have encroached on the gorilla's territory, clearing lush forests for timber and creating fields for agriculture and livestock. Poaching occurs as well, and the loss of even a few of these gorillas has a detrimental effect on such a small population – there are only an estimated 200 to 300 individuals left in the wild.

Conservation efforts are underway to protect Cross River gorillas by tackling forest loss and poaching. Organizations are working with logging companies, the Cameroon Ministry of Forest and Wildlife, and local communities to manage the gorillas' forest home more sustainably and protect wildlife corridors and waterways.

| | |
|---:|:---|
| Population trend | **Decreasing** |
| Habitats | **Forest** |
| Distribution | **Southeast Madagascar** |
| Threats | **Deforestation, mining** |

**EX** **EW** **CR** **EN** **VU** **NT** **LC**

# Thomas' dwarf lemur

*Cheirogaleus thomasi*

Thomas' dwarf lemurs make their home in the Sainte Luce Littoral Forest in Madagascar, an island renowned for its incredible biodiversity. They are nocturnal, live in large groups, and feed on fruit and flowers. Like all lemurs, they help the forest by dispersing seeds. However, the littoral forest habitat they rely on is disappearing – only 10 percent remains. This is due to deforestation and mining for natural resources. As deforestation increases, creating more forest fragments, these animals have less space to live in. They are unable to cross the open land between the forest patches, therefore individual populations are becoming increasingly isolated.

The People's Trust for Endangered Species is funding work to safeguard and reconnect the Sainte Luce Littoral Forest. Working with their partners, SEED Madagascar, they are planting habitat corridors between legally protected forest fragments. Many other endemic plants and animals that are unable to disperse between isolated patches of habitat will also benefit.

| | |
|---|---|
| Population trend | **Decreasing** |
| Habitats | **Forest, shrubland, wetlands, caves** |
| Distribution | **Sardinia (Italy)** |
| Threats | **Habitat loss, pollution, drought, predation, disease** |

EX EW CR **EN** VU NT LC
▲

# Sardinian newt

*Euproctus platycephalus*

Also known as the Sardinian brook salamander, this amphibian lives in the mountainous east side of the island of Sardinia in the Mediterranean Sea. It prefers calm water, including slow-moving streams, lakes, ponds, and even cave systems. When on land, and during hibernation, it can be found in the undergrowth and under stones, usually close to water. As waterways and ponds become polluted or dry up due to pressure from tourism, they are losing places to live. This species is also under threat from habitat fragmentation and predation by introduced trout. To make their situation worse, the newts are affected by a parasitic disease, which can kill them.

The Gola di Gorropu, a national park regarded as the Grand Canyon of Europe, has been designated as a Site of Community Importance under the EU Habitats Directive. The IUCN has recommended the removal of trout from this habitat to help salamander populations recover.

| Population trend | **Decreasing** |
|---|---|
| Habitats | **Grassland, marine** |
| Distribution | **East Canada to West Europe and North Russia** |
| Threats | **Overfishing, climate change, pollution, invasive species** |

EX  EW  CR  EN  **VU**  NT  LC
▲

# Atlantic puffin

*Fratercula arctica*

These "clowns of the sea" display brightly colored beaks and feet during the mating season. Their beaks are serrated with an extra bone at the tip, which they use to catch and carry multiple fish, such as herring, hake, and sand eels. Puffin couples often use old rabbit burrows in rocky cliffs to nest. They return to the same nesting site each year, and may even return to the same burrow. Both parents take turns incubating the egg.

They are classified as Vulnerable because overfishing by humans is causing a shortage of food for adults to feed their young. The climate crisis is having an adverse impact, since puffins are adapted for hunting fish that live in cold waters. Global heating also causes rising sea levels, which could flood puffins' breeding grounds.

Organizations, including the Marine Conservation Society, are working towards better protection of puffin marine habitats in the UK and the better management of fisheries that affect puffin prey.

| Population trend | **Unknown** |
| --- | --- |
| Habitats | **Marine** |
| Distribution | **Worldwide (except shallow waters and high-latitude polar regions)** |
| Threats | **Bycatch, pollution, disturbance** |

EX EW CR EN **VU** NT LC
▲

# Cuvier's beaked whale

*Ziphius cavirostris*

Cuvier's beaked whales hold the record for the deepest and longest dive for any mammal (nearly two miles/three kilometers) to reach deep-dwelling prey, such as squid. Cuvier's have flipper pockets, a special adaptation for diving that allows them to tuck their flippers in and make their bodies super-streamlined. Other than the pair of teeth in adult males, beaked whales are generally toothless and are thought to use suction to catch their food. When they come close to the surface they are vulnerable to being caught in nets. They suffer decompression sickness, or the bends, if they are frightened by artificial noise and surface too quickly. Tragically, mass strandings of Cuvier's beaked whales have occurred around the world, following naval sonar exercises.

Marine conservationists are campaigning for stronger laws to protect whales and dolphins and create cleaner, healthier seas. They are working with scientists and fishermen to find innovative ways for fisheries to operate, and to develop and use safer technologies.

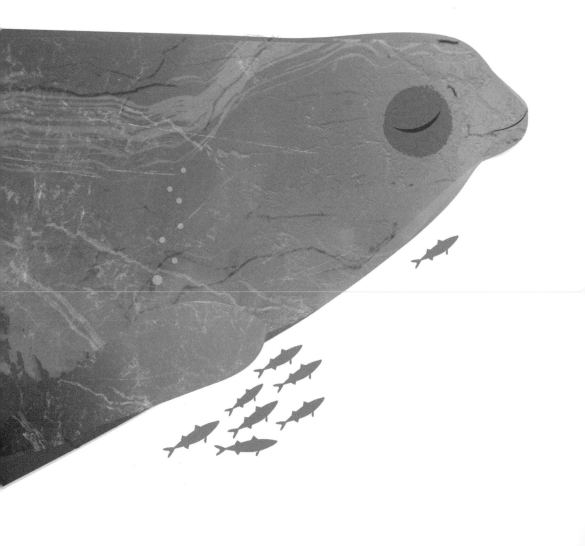

| | |
|---|---|
| Population trend | **Decreasing** |
| Habitats | **Forest** |
| Distribution | **Colombia, Ecuador, Panama** |
| Threats | **Hunting, habitat loss, deforestation** |

EX  EW  CR  **EN**  VU  NT  LC

# Brown-headed spider monkey
*Ateles fusciceps*

With their long limbs and slender body, these monkeys are perfectly suited to leaping through the tree canopy. Their long, prehensile tail is used as a fifth limb and can support their whole body. Like all spider monkeys, they see the world in color, which is useful for spotting the ripest fruit among the foliage. They are only found in the rainforests of Ecuador, Colombia, and Panama, where they are important seed dispersers – some timber fruits cannot germinate until they have been softened through the process of being eaten by these monkeys. With a population loss of 80 percent, they are one of the 25 most endangered primates. They are threatened by habitat loss and fragmentation, as well as being hunted for their meat and fur.

Through research, environmental education, and community development programs, organizations are trying to protect the land these monkeys depend on. Ecuador's Ministry of Environment Socio Bosque project offers economic incentives to forest owners who agree to protect biodiversity.

| | |
|---|---|
| Population trend | **Decreasing** |
| Habitats | **Forest** |
| Distribution | **Madagascar** |
| Threats | **Habitat loss** |

EX EW CR **EN** VU NT LC
▲

# Helmet vanga
*Euryceros prevostii*

The helmet vanga bird lives in the humid rainforest of north-eastern Madagascar. It is the second largest of the vanga birds. There are around 20 species on the island. Vanga beaks come in all shapes and sizes, and with its impressive brilliant-blue beak, the helmet vanga is the "toucan" of the family. This bird is an ambush hunter, catching large insects from above. It also eats millipedes, frogs, and lizards. Most vangas nest in pairs, building cup-shaped nests, using twigs, bark, roots, and leaves. It is threatened with extinction because its home is being cleared for agriculture and forestry. It is likely to be severely affected by the climate crisis.

BirdLife International is carrying out surveys to record population numbers in both protected and unprotected areas. They are trying to improve awareness of conservation and the implications of widespread forest loss among local people.

| | |
|---|---|
| Population trend | **Decreasing** |
| Habitats | **Shrubland, grassland, desert** |
| Distribution | **Argentina, Chile** |
| Threats | **Habitat loss, hunting, disease, predation** |

EX EW CR EN VU NT LC

▲

# Pichi

*Zaedyus pichiy*

The pichi, or dwarf armadillo, is found only in the scrubby grasslands, sandy plains, and dunes of South Argentina and Chile. It is mostly nocturnal, about nine inches (23 centimeters) long, with a tail of about four inches (11 centimeters), and spends its time burrowing underground. It feeds on termites, beetles, vegetation, and small animals. It is the only armadillo to hibernate. Armadillo is a Spanish word and means "little armored one." Its hard shell, known as the carapace, is made of bone and hard tissue, and is used as a defense against potential predators. If threatened, the dwarf armadillo will run and hide underground. As farming intensifies across their habitat, numbers are declining. Pichi are killed by dogs and cats.

More data is needed about the distribution of dwarf armadillo populations. Conservationists are providing outreach materials about armadillos to local communities to promote conservation through sustainable use and responsible hunting practices.

| | |
|---|---|
| Population trend | **Decreasing** |
| Habitats | **Savanna, shrubland, grassland, wetlands, rocky areas** |
| Distribution | **Africa, Asia, Middle East, Southern Europe** |
| Threats | **Hunting, poisoning, disturbance, pollution** |

EX EW CR **EN** VU NT LC
▲

# Egyptian vulture

*Neophron percnopterus*

The Egyptian vulture's image was once used as an Ancient Egyptian hieroglyph and represented the letter "a." It was also a symbol of royal protection, life, and death. It is an intelligent species and uses tools such as stones to crack open large eggs, and twigs to gather wool to line its nest. As a scavenger, it feeds on carrion and plays an important role in the ecosystem, disposing of dead animal carcasses quickly, thereby stopping the spread of disease. Collisions with power lines, hunting, intentional poisoning, lead accumulation from ingesting gunshot in carcasses, and pesticide accumulation are all taking a toll on populations of Egyptian vultures. Their numbers have declined worldwide. In Europe, the species has declined by over 50 percent in the past 50 years.

Conservationists, researchers, and representatives from 33 countries are developing an International Egyptian Vulture Flyway Action Plan. Education programs are being established to discourage hunting, and reintroductions are taking place across Europe to help this endangered bird.

| | |
|---:|:---|
| Population trend | **Decreasing** |
| Habitats | **Wetlands, marine** |
| Distribution | **East and Southeast Asia, Indonesia** |
| Threats | **Bycatch, wildlife trade, pollution, climate change, habitat loss** |

EX EW CR **EN** VU NT LC

# Irrawaddy dolphin
*Orcaella brevirostris*

Irrawaddy dolphins are found in coastal areas and three rivers: the Ayeyarwady (Myanmar), the Mahakam (Indonesian Borneo), and the Mekong (East and Southeast Asia). These charismatic dolphins have unusually expressive faces, thanks to moveable lips and creases around their necks that enable them to move their heads in all directions. When socializing and fishing, they can spit spouts of water from their mouths into the air. But fishing is a problem: irrawaddy dolphins are drowning in large, vertical gill nets and have fallen victim to the explosions used to blast fish out of the water. They have also been taken and put into captivity.

In 2004, marine conservation organizations and TRAFFIC, the world's largest wildlife trade monitoring network, supported a ban on the international live trade of irrawaddy dolphins. As well as ending captivity, conservationists are trying to create healthy seas and prevent deaths in nets.

| | |
|---|---|
| Population trend | **Decreasing** |
| Habitats | **Forest, savanna, shrubland, grassland, desert** |
| Distribution | **Sub-Saharan Africa** |
| Threats | **Habitat loss, hunting, conflict** |

EX　EW　CR　EN　VU　NT　LC
▲

# African lion

*Panthera leo*

Lions are sociable animals and live in groups called prides. Of all the big cats, male and female lions are the only ones that look distinctly different from one another. Only adult males have a mane, which extends down the neck and chest and is believed to be a way of showing status and strength, and to attract females. As top predators, they play a crucial role in keeping a healthy balance among other animals, especially zebra, deer, and wildebeest. Data released in 2015 revealed that numbers had plummeted by 42 percent over 21 years. Habitat loss and conflict with humans both play a part in their decline. As human populations continue to expand into lion territory, this is leading to clashes between cats and people. If a lion attacks a farmer's livestock, often the lion is killed in retaliation. Hunting is also rife throughout Africa.

Conservationists are working to address traditional lion killings in local cultures, mitigate human-lion conflict, address bush-meat poaching, and reduce trophy hunting.

| | |
|---|---|
| Population trend | **Decreasing** |
| Habitats | **Wetlands, marine** |
| Distribution | **Brazil, Colombia, Ecuador, Peru** |
| Threats | **Hunting, bycatch, pollution** |

EX  EW  CR  EN  **VU**  NT  LC
▲

# Amazonian manatee

*Trichechus inunguis*

The Amazonian manatee is one of three manatee, or "sea cow," species. Together with the dugong, they are the only plant-eating marine mammals in the world. The Amazonian manatee feeds on aquatic grasses, water lettuce, and hyacinth in lagoons, oxbows, and blackwater lakes in the Amazon River Basin. They are entirely aquatic and never leave their freshwater home. Because they inhabit murky waters, it is difficult to get an accurate population estimate. They are still being hunted for their meat and skin, and because they are slow-moving, docile animals, they are easy to catch. Like other marine species, they get caught in fishing nets and are affected by pollution. This problem is especially prevalent in Ecuador, where increasing oil exploration has caused oil spillages.

As well as international conservation programs, the Amazon Rescue Center, located in the heart of the Amazon, is dedicated to rescuing and rehabilitating orphaned Amazonian manatees, as well as delivering environmental education.

| | |
|---|---|
| Population trend | **Decreasing** |
| Habitats | **Desert** |
| Distribution | **Northern China, Southern Mongolia** |
| Threats | **Habitat loss, hunting, hybridization** |

EX  EW  **CR**  EN  VU  NT  LC

# Bactrian camel

*Camelus ferus*

Wild Bactrian camels live in the harsh landscape of the Gobi Desert. Bushy eyebrows and two rows of long eyelashes protect their eyes from the sand, and their nostrils close to keep grains from entering their noses. Big, flat feet help them cross the rocky terrain and shifting dunes. Unlike their Arabian relatives, Bactrian camels have two humps, rather than one, to store fat, which can be converted to water and energy when food is scarce. They can also survive on water saltier than seawater, something that no other mammal in the world can do. These remarkable animals are listed as Critically Endangered because of interbreeding and hybridization with the domesticated Bactrian camels. They are losing their home to mining and industrial development.

The Wild Camel Foundation is working with government and local authorities in China and Mongolia to try to protect camels in the wild. They have established the Lop Nur Wild Camel National Nature Reserve.

| | |
|---|---|
| Population trend | **Decreasing** |
| Habitats | **Forest, shrubland, grassland, caves** |
| Distribution | **Europe, Middle East, North Africa** |
| Threats | **Disturbance, insecticides, habitat loss** |

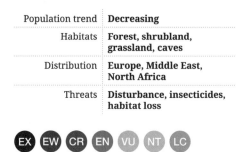

EX  EW  CR  EN  VU  NT  **LC**
▲

# Lesser horseshoe bat

*Rhinolophus hipposideros*

The lesser horseshoe is one of over 1,200 bat species in the world. When resting inside barns, churches, and stables, it hangs from its feet with its wings wrapped around its body. It has a characteristically fleshy nose or "noseleaf" shaped like a horseshoe, which it uses in echolocation. Midges, caddis flies, lacewings, and other flying insects form the main part of its diet. From September to April, lesser horseshoe bats hibernate in caves, mines, tunnels, and cellars. These are all quiet places that maintain a constant temperature of between 40 and 52 degrees Fahrenheit (five and eleven degrees centigrade) and have a high humidity.

The decline of the lesser horseshoe bat in the UK is due to disturbance to their roosting and wintering sites, and habitat loss through intensive farming. Several UK conservation charities, including the Bat Conservation Trust, are working with farmers and landowners to protect bat colonies and to manage land more sensitively for wildlife.

| | |
|---:|:---|
| Population trend | **Decreasing** |
| Habitats | **Marine** |
| Distribution | **Worldwide** |
| Threats | **Bycatch, overfishing** |

EX EW **CR** EN VU NT LC
▲

# Great hammerhead

*Sphyrna mokarran*

The largest of all nine hammerhead species, the great hammerhead can reach up to 20 feet (six meters) long. It has an almost-straight, hammer-shaped head (known as a cephalofoil), which has a prominent indentation in the middle. Great hammerheads glide effortlessly through tropical and warm temperate seas, and specialize in hunting and eating large stingrays. Their wide-set eyes give them a wider field of view than most other sharks, and as their highly specialized sensory organs are spread over their T-shaped head, they are can scan the ocean floor for food more thoroughly.

Although they are not targeted directly by commercial fisheries, great hammerheads are a bycatch species of tropical long-line and drift net fisheries. Their large fins are highly valued for shark fin soup, which is served in parts of Asia. They are also a popular fish with recreational anglers due to their large size. No conservation measures specifically protect the great hammerhead, but shark finning is now banned in the United States, Australia, and the European Union.

| | |
|---|---|
| Population trend | **Decreasing** |
| Habitats | **Forest, shrubland, rocky areas, caves** |
| Distribution | **Algeria, Gibraltar, Morocco** |
| Threats | **Wildlife trade, deforestation** |

EX EW CR **EN** VU NT LC
▲

# Barbary macaque
*Macaca sylvanus*

With its thick fur coat, this tailless monkey can tolerate the cold, as well as the hot, dry weather in the Atlas Mountains of Algeria and Morocco. It is the only primate in North Africa and has an important role in keeping forests healthy by spreading seeds. From fir and mixed forests to sheer cliff faces, the monkeys live in groups, ranging from 30 to 80 individuals, moving together to forage for food. Bonds are formed within the troops, and hours are spent grooming. Barbarys often "teeth chatter" to one another as a friendly greeting. They are threatened by habitat destruction and degradation, as well as the capture of infants for the pet trade.

Projects are underway to help local communities to protect these animals, to use the forest in a sustainable way, and to stop the capture of infant macaques to be used in the tourist trade or sold as pets.

| Population trend | **Decreasing** |
| Habitats | **Forest, shrubland, grassland** |
| Distribution | **Europe** |
| Threats | **Habitat loss** |

EX  EW  CR  **EN**  VU  NT  LC
▲

# Large blue
*Phengaris arion*

The large blue is a fairly small butterfly, but the largest and rarest of Britain's blue butterflies, and the only one with black spots on the upper side of the forewing. It can be found in a wide variety of habitats in Europe, including coastal cliffs, limestone gorges, and alpine pastures. This butterfly has a remarkable life cycle and has developed a close association with wild thyme and a species of red ant. When the caterpillars are about one-eighth of an inch (four millimeters) long, they drop to the ground and use a special "honey" gland to attract red ants. Fooled into thinking the caterpillar is an ant grub, the ants carry them into their nests, where the caterpillars then feast on the ant grubs they find there. Changes in farming practices last century caused this particular red ant to vanish. This had a knock-on effect for large blue butterflies: by 1979, large blues were extinct in the UK.

Reintroduction programs and new grazing regimes brought back both the ants and the butterflies. They need wild thyme, growing among short turf on sheltered sites, to survive.

| | |
|---:|:---|
| Population trend | **Decreasing** |
| Habitats | **Forest** |
| Distribution | **Madagascar** |
| Threats | **Habitat loss, hunting** |

EX  EW  CR  EN  **VU**  NT  LC
▲

# Fosa
*Cryptoprocta ferox*

The fosa is a cat-like animal, closely related to the mongoose family, and found in the quieter parts of the forests of Madagascar. It is both tree and ground dwelling. It has short, reddish-brown, smooth and relatively dense fur, and a tail almost as long as its body. It is active by day and night and preys on most forest animals, including lemurs, rodents, and reptiles. As the island's top predator, it plays an important role in balancing the ecosystem. Fosas are directly affected by the widespread destruction of Madagascar's native forests for selective logging and the conversion of forest to agricultural land and pasture.

Local people are being trained in techniques of improved poultry farming to help them become less reliant on bush-meat hunting. Information and awareness campaigns highlighting the importance of fosa are underway to involve local communities in the conservation of this species.

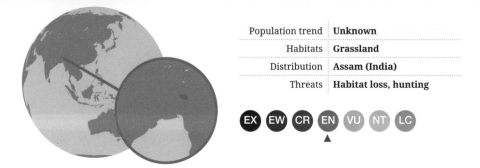

| Population trend | **Unknown** |
| --- | --- |
| Habitats | **Grassland** |
| Distribution | **Assam (India)** |
| Threats | **Habitat loss, hunting** |

EX EW CR **EN** VU NT LC
▲

# Pygmy hog
*Porcula salvania*

The pygmy hog is the smallest pig in the world. With short legs and a streamlined body, it is well adapted to pushing through tall, dense grassland in the southern Himalayan foothills. Active during the day, it forages for roots, tubers, insects, rodents, and small reptiles. It is one of the very few mammals that build its own home, or nest, complete with a "roof." While traveling, family groups move in single file, with an adult at each end. Pygmy hogs used to be widespread throughout Nepal and North Bengal, but human expansion and intensive farming has destroyed much of their natural habitat. They are now endangered, with fewer than 250 individuals left in the wild.

The Pygmy Hog Conservation program was established in 1995 and is raising local community awareness and conducting behavioral studies, field surveys, and a successful breeding and reintroduction program.

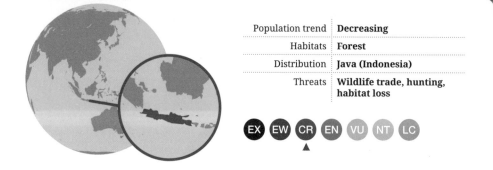

| | |
|---:|:---|
| Population trend | **Decreasing** |
| Habitats | **Forest** |
| Distribution | **Java (Indonesia)** |
| Threats | **Wildlife trade, hunting, habitat loss** |

EX · EW · **CR** · EN · VU · NT · LC

# Javan slow loris
*Nycticebus javanicus*

The Javan slow loris is a small, nocturnal primate. It travels through the trees using slow, hand-over-hand movements in search of flowers, nectar, fruit, insects, and reptiles. It can also eat tree gum, which other animals cannot. Huge eyes enable it to see at night, and as it moves through the forest, it performs the vital service of pollinating flowers and eating pest insects. It is the only venomous primate and produces a toxin in the glands on the inside of its elbows to deter potential predators. The Javan slow loris is one of the world's most endangered primates, suffering a decline of at least 80 percent over the past 24 years. These animals are illegally captured and sold as pets. Their forest homes are also being destroyed, as they are converted to farmland.

The Little Fireface Project is dedicated to protecting the remaining population through research, education, and outreach, helping local communities to become the stewards of these special animals.

| | |
|---|---|
| Population trend | **Stable** |
| Habitats | **Forest, grassland, wetlands** |
| Distribution | **Asia, Europe** |
| Threats | **Predation, habitat loss, pollution, competition** |

EX  EW  CR  EN  VU  NT  **LC**
▲

# European water vole

*Arvicola amphibius*

Known as Ratty in Kenneth Grahame's classic children's tale, *The Wind in the Willows*, the European water vole digs its burrows in steep, grassy banks along slow-moving rivers, streams, and canals. In spring and summer, it nibbles on grasses, reeds, and sedges, and in fall and winter, it gnaws on roots, tree bark, and fruit.

Although water voles are classified as Least Concern by the IUCN, in the UK they have experienced the most catastrophic decline of any mammal. It is thought that in 90 percent of the sites in England, Scotland and Wales where populations were previously found, they have now been lost entirely. This occurred in just a couple of decades. The main culprits are habitat loss and fragmentation, as well as the introduction of the American mink.

The People's Trust for Endangered Species has funded 45 conservation projects for water voles since 1997 and runs the National Water Vole Monitoring program.

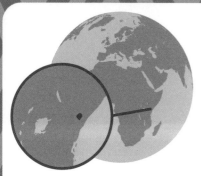

| | |
|---|---|
| Population trend | **Decreasing** |
| Habitats | **Savanna, shrubland, grassland** |
| Distribution | **Kenya** |
| Threats | **Habitat loss, drought, disease** |

EX EW **CR** EN VU NT LC
▲

# Hirola

*Beatragus hunteri*

The hirola lives in the short grasslands and semi-arid bushland of Kenya. It is tawny or tan-brown and has long, sharp horns. Around its eyes are white markings that resemble spectacles. Dark glands under its eyes are used to mark its territories, giving them the name "four-eyed antelope." The hirola is the world's most endangered antelope, with fewer than 500 animals remaining. The shockingly low numbers are largely due to habitat loss, as the grassland they depend on has steadily disappeared. The hirola has suffered drastic declines due to over-hunting in the past, and a lack of effective protection leaves it vulnerable to poaching. It is also vulnerable to disease, drought, and competition with livestock.

Conservationists are working to increase grassland for the hirola, and to improve protection and local livelihoods by engaging communities through education and outreach.

| | |
|---:|:---|
| Population trend | **Decreasing** |
| Habitats | **Grassland, rocky areas, marine** |
| Distribution | **Indian and South Atlantic Oceans** |
| Threats | **Overfishing, pollution, climate change, predation** |

EX  EW  CR  **EN**  VU  NT  LC

# Northern rockhopper penguin

*Eudyptes moseleyi*

Rockhoppers are the smallest of the crested penguins. As their name suggests, they hop across rocks when they move on land. Northern rockhoppers spend a lot of time in the ocean waters of Antarctica, diving for krill, fish, and other sea life, such as squid and octopus. When it is time to have their young, they move to the shores of Gough Island and the Tristan da Cunha archipelago, forming vast breeding colonies. Unlike other species of penguin, they can become quite aggressive. When fighting, they will slap each other with their flippers.

The breeding population of northern rockhoppers on Gough Island has declined by 90 percent since the 1950s. Oil spills, commercial fishing, and introduced animals have affected populations. Changes in sea-surface temperatures are another contributing factor. In 2016, Project Pinnamin was established to enable conservationists to study the marine ecology, breeding biology, and survival of the northern rockhopper penguin.

| | |
|---|---|
| Population trend | **Decreasing** |
| Habitats | **Forest, shrubland, grassland, wetlands, rocky areas** |
| Distribution | **East Asia, West Europe** |
| Threats | **Habitat loss, persecution** |

EX  EW  CR  EN  VU  NT  **LC**
▲

# European common adder
*Vipera berus*

The common adder is easily recognized by a dark, continuous zigzag stripe along its back. The background color varies from gray-white in the male to shades of brown in the female. The adder eats frogs, young birds, and small mammals. It bears its young alive, and between six and 20 are born in August or early September. Adders tend to be restricted to sunny, open habitats, such as heath and moorland. The loss and fragmentation of these wild places, as well as direct persecution, has led to the disappearance of adders. Within the last century they have experienced a widespread decline.

Adders are protected by law in the UK. It is illegal to intentionally kill, injure, or trade in them. Many UK conservation organizations are carrying out surveys and habitat management to conserve adder populations.

| Population trend | **Decreasing** |
| --- | --- |
| Habitats | **Forest, savanna, shrubland** |
| Distribution | **Africa, Asia, Europe** |
| Threats | **Habitat loss, climate change** |

EX EW CR EN VU NT **LC**

# Spotted flycatcher

*Muscicapa striata*

Although a little drab to look at, the aerial agility of the spotted flycatcher are impressive. It can intercept fast-flying insects, such as damselflies, bees, and wasps, in mid-air. Spotted flycatchers are migratory birds, spending the winter in Africa and arriving in the UK to breed from late April to early May. Once considered a common garden nesting species, it is now disappearing. There has been a decline of 87 percent since 1970. Decreases in the annual survival rates of birds in their first year are most likely to be causing this. Deteriorating woodlands, unfavorable conditions, either on wintering grounds or along migration routes, could be to blame, as well as a decline in flying insects.

The British Trust for Ornithology (BTO) is using tracking devices and the support of volunteers to follow birds as they migrate from the UK. This will help to identify their wintering grounds and the areas that the birds use as stopover sites en route.

| | |
|---:|:---|
| Population trend | **Decreasing** |
| Habitats | **Forest, savanna, shrubland, grassland, wetlands** |
| Distribution | **Africa, Asia, Middle East** |
| Threats | **Hunting, conflict, habitat loss** |

EX EW CR EN VU **NT** LC

# Striped hyena
*Hyaena hyaena*

Striped hyenas are the smallest of the three hyena species and have vertical stripes on their flanks and legs. When threatened, the mane that extends down the middle of their back can be made to stand up, which makes the hyena appear larger and more intimidating. They are efficient predators and carrion scavengers. With unique immune systems, they are able to digest rotten meat that other animals cannot. They help to keep the ecosystem healthy by removing bacteria that could leach into the soil and water. Although the population size is quite large, striped hyenas are scattered over wide areas and isolated from each other. Like many carnivores, they are considered a pest species by humans, as they prey on livestock. This often results in retaliatory killings by farmers.

Work is underway to improve people's negative attitude to hyenas. This involves on-the-ground research and helping local communities to protect their livestock from potential attacks.

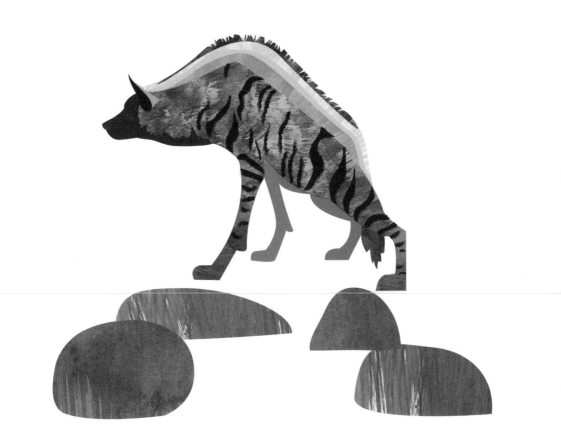

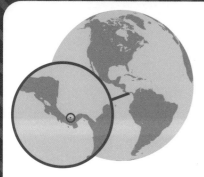

| Population trend | **Decreasing** |
| --- | --- |
| Habitats | **Forest** |
| Distribution | **Isla Escudo de Veraguas (Panama)** |
| Threats | **Habitat loss, hunting, wildlife trade** |

EX EW **CR** EN VU NT LC
▲

# Pygmy three-toed sloth

*Bradypus pygmaeus*

The pygmy three-toed sloth is found only on the tiny island of Escudo de Veraguas, off the coast of Panama. It is the smallest of the three-toed sloths. It feeds on the leaves of the red mangrove trees in which it lives. Since it is a slow-moving animal, its main defense is to blend in with its environment. A green algae found in its fur is thought to be symbiotic, providing convincing camouflage. Although their island home is uninhabited, it is being destroyed daily, as local fishermen cut down the mangroves for charcoal and timber. The numbers of seasonal residents are growing, increasing the pressure from small-scale logging, fishing, and littering. There is also a looming threat of large-scale tourism, which could cause sloths to be taken into captivity.

The global conservation initiative, EDGE is carrying out educational programs to increase local awareness, establish sustainable land management, and support local authorities in enforcing sloth protection.

| | |
|---|---|
| Population trend | **Decreasing** |
| Habitats | **Forest** |
| Distribution | **Canada, United States** |
| Threats | **Habitat loss, hunting** |

EX EW CR EN VU NT **LC**

# American marten

*Martes americana*

The solitary and nocturnal American marten is a cat-sized member of the weasel family and has a long, bushy tail. It is the only mustelid with semi-retractable claws, which it uses to climb and travel along the branches of trees. It has a characteristic yellow bib by its throat, set against dark brown fur, which grows longer and silkier in the winter. The American marten is lighter in color than its European cousin and has a gray head. These martens spend a lot of their time in the trees, but they do most of their hunting on the ground, feeding on small mammals, carrion, birds, insects, and fruit. As predators, American martens help to keep the forest ecosystem healthy.

The American marten population declined due to the fur trade. Numerous protection measures and reintroduction efforts have allowed the population to increase, but habitat loss is still a problem.

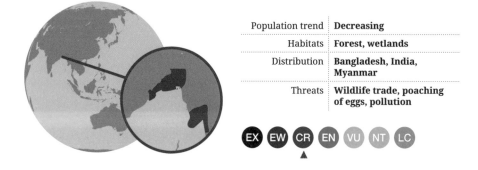

| Population trend | **Decreasing** |
|---|---|
| Habitats | **Forest, wetlands** |
| Distribution | **Bangladesh, India, Myanmar** |
| Threats | **Wildlife trade, poaching of eggs, pollution** |

EX EW **CR** EN VU NT LC

# Northern river terrapin

*Batagur baska*

The Sundarbans mangrove forest, famed for its wildlife, spans India and Bangladesh and is home to northern river terrapins. They are one of Asia's biggest freshwater turtles and feed on waterside plants and clams. Even though large areas are now protected, the long history of exploitation and lack of enforcement in both countries has resulted in catastrophe for these turtles. With no record of them in the wild for over a decade in Bangladesh, and even longer in India, northern river terrapins are the world's second most endangered turtle. It is estimated that there are fewer than 100 adults in captive collections across the globe.

The Turtle Survival Alliance and Sundarban Tiger Reserve are creating a conservation strategy. A breeding program has successfully been established and reintroductions and monitoring will follow. If wild populations can be found while releasing new animals, there is a chance of restoring this creature back to the wild.

| | |
|---|---|
| Population trend | **Decreasing** |
| Habitats | **Forest, savanna, shrubland, desert** |
| Distribution | **Africa, Asia, Europe** |
| Threats | **Hybridization, disease, accidental persecution** |

EX EW CR EN VU NT LC
▲

# Wild cat

*Felis silvestris*

Although similar in appearance to a large tabby cat, the wild cat is a fierce hunter with a thick, banded tail with a black, blunt tip. Also, their fur is thicker and they have a heavier skull with a more angular jaw for seizing and crunching live prey. Often referred to as the "tiger of the Highlands," they are one of Scotland's last remaining natural predators and play an important role in a healthy ecosystem, controlling rats, rabbits, and other small mammals. The last remaining populations of wild cats in the Highlands are now critically endangered. They are primarily threatened by hybridization with feral domestic cats, which transmit diseases to the Scottish wild cat. They are also at risk of persecution.

Scottish Wildcat Action and land management partners are providing training in wild cat identification. Captive breeding and reintroduction programs are underway. Promoting responsible cat ownership to ensure that cats are tagged, neutered, and disease-free is also important.

| | |
|---:|:---|
| Population trend | **Decreasing** |
| Habitats | **Marine** |
| Distribution | **Southeast Asia** |
| Threats | **Wildlife trade, bycatch, habitat loss** |

EX EW CR EN **VU** NT LC
▲

# Tiger tail seahorse

*Hippocampus comes*

Only seahorses belong to the genus *Hippocampus*, from the Greek words for "horse" (*hippos*) and "sea monster" (*campus*). Like its feline namesake, the tiger tail seahorse is often active at night, and inhabits the coral reefs, mangroves and estuaries of Southeast Asia. All seahorses are masters of camouflage, changing color to blend in with their surroundings and during courtship displays and daily greetings. Only the male becomes pregnant, carrying eggs in a brood pouch, before giving birth to live young. Seahorses are important predators on sea- and riverbed-dwelling organisms, helping to maintain the health of their habitat. Besides the wildlife trade, tiger tail seahorses are threatened by the destruction of their home through human activities. Many seahorses are also caught accidentally in fishing nets, particularly in trawl nets intended to catch shrimps.

Through a combination of research, citizen science, trade and policy work, and marine-protected areas, Project Seahorse is trying to ensure that seahorse populations and their habitats are healthy and well managed.

| | |
|---:|:---|
| Population trend | **Decreasing** |
| Habitats | **Forest** |
| Distribution | **Madagascar** |
| Threats | **Habitat loss, hunting** |

EX EW CR EN VU NT LC

# Indri

*Indri indri*

The indri is one of the largest lemur species, weighing an impressive 13 to 22 pounds (six to ten kilograms) in adulthood. Restricted to the northern and central rainforests of East Madagascar, indri live in bonded, male-female pairs with their offspring. Among the most unique and spectacular characteristics of the indri is its song: a high, mournful wail used to defend territories and maintain family unity up in the tree canopy. Indri forage on young leaves, fruit, and flowers. In Malagasy, indri are called *babakoto* and are considered by many to be the ancestor of humans. Although many believe that the indri are sacred and shouldn't be harmed, hunting pressure and habitat loss have made them critically endangered.

Several international organizations, including Duke Lemur Center, are running research and conservation programs in collaboration with Malagasy people to establish more sustainable ways of life and protecting their natural resources.

# Get Involved

You don't have to be a conservationist to make a positive difference for wildlife. There are many small steps you can take to tread lighter on the planet and also lend your support to existing organizations and projects.

You can find out more about conservation issues and initiatives, and how to get involved, on the following websites:

## Global Conservation Organizations and Initiatives

**Birdlife International**
www.birdlife.org
A global partnership of organizations, working to conserve birds, their habitats and global biodiversity.

**Born Free Foundation**
www.bornfree.org
An international wildlife charity that campaigns to keep wildlife in the wild.

**EDGE**
www.edgeofexistence.org
The Edge of Existence program identifies and protects the world's most Evolutionarily Distinct and Globally Endangered species.

**International Union for the Conservation of Nature (IUCN)**
www.iucn.org
The most up-to-date source of facts and figures on globally threatened species.

**People's Trust for Endangered Species (PTES)**
www.ptes.org
PTES promotes the conservation of rare or declining species and habitats in the UK and worldwide.

**Rainforest Alliance**
www.rainforest-alliance.org
An alliance protecting forests and improving the livelihoods of farmers and forest communities.

**TRAFFIC**
www.traffic.org
Wildlife trade monitoring network that ensures that trade in wild plants and animals is not a threat to the conservation of nature.

**Wildlife Conservation Research Unit (WILDCRU)**
www.wildcru.org
WILDCRU works on practical solutions to conservation problems through original scientific research. (It is part of the Zoology Department of Oxford University.)

**World Land Trust**
www.worldlandtrust.org
The trust protects threatened habitats worldwide.

**World Wildlife Fund (WWF)**
www.worldwildlife.org
The world's leading independent nature conservation organization.

# UK Species-specific Organizations and Projects

**Amphibian and Reptile Conservation**
www.arc-trust.org

**Bat Conservation Trust**
www.bats.org.uk

**BugLife**
www.buglife.org.uk

**British Trust for Ornithology (BTO)**
www.bto.org

**Bumblebee Conservation Trust**
www.bumblebeeconservation.org

**Butterfly Conservation**
www.butterfly-conservation.org

**Marine Conservation Society (MCS)**
www.mcsuk.org

**Red Squirrels United**
www.redsquirrelsunited.org.uk

**Royal Society for the Protection of Birds (RSPB)**
www.rspb.org.uk

**Scottish Wildcat Action**
www.scottishwildcataction.org

**Shark Trust**
www.sharktrust.org

**Surfers Against Sewage**
www.sas.org.uk

**The Wildlife Trusts**
www.wildlifetrusts.org

**The Woodland Trust**
www.woodlandtrust.org.uk

# Worldwide Species-specific Organizations and Projects

**Bear Conservation**
www.bearconservation.org.uk

**Caspian Seal Project**
www.caspianseal.org

**Cross River Gorilla Project**
www.crossrivergorillaproject.co.uk

**Duke Lemur Center**
www.lemur.duke.edu

**Egyptian Vulture Flyway Action Plan (EVFAP)**
www.lifeneophron.eu

**Ethiopian Wolf Conservation Programme (EWCP)**
www.ethiopianwolf.org

**Galápagos Conservation Trust**
www.galapagosconservation.org.uk

**Giraffe Conservation Foundation (GCF)**
www.giraffeconservation.org

**International Crane Foundation**
www.savingcranes.org

**Kakapo Recovery**
www.doc.govt.nz/our-work/
kakapo-recovery

**Little Fireface Project**
www.nocturama.org

**Orangutan Foundation**
www.orangutan.org.uk

**Pallas's Cat International Conservation Alliance (PICA)**
www.pallascats.org

**Project Pinnamin (northern rockhopper penguin)**
www.rzss.org.uk

**Project Seahorse**
www.projectseahorse.org

**Pygmy Hog Conservation Programme**
www.pygmyhog.org

**Saiga Conservation Alliance**
www.saiga-conservation.org

**Save the Tasmanian Devil Program**
www.tassiedevil.com.au

**SEED Madagascar**
www.madagascar.co.uk

**The Turtle Survival Alliance**
www.turtlesurvival.org

**Wild Camel Protection Foundation**
www.wildcamels.com

# Glossary

**Archipelago**
A group of islands

**Biodiversity**
The variety of plant and animal life found in the world or a particular habitat

**Bycatch**
Unwanted fish (or other marine species) caught while fishing for a different species

**Captive breeding**
Breeding endangered species in zoos and sanctuaries to help build a healthy population of the animals

**Carrion**
The decaying flesh of dead animals

**Climate change (also known as global heating or global warming)**
The process of our planet heating up, which is making our weather more extreme and unpredictable

**Conservation**
The careful protection of something, such as a species or habitat

**Deforestation**
Clearing wide areas of trees

**Distribution (of a species)**
The places where a species is found

**DNA profiling (also known as genetic profiling)**
Studying DNA samples taken from animals to understand more about their genetic make-up

**Ecosystem**
A community of living and non-living things in one area

**El Niño**
Natural events (e.g. heavy rainfall or drought) that take place every two to five years, caused by rising temperatures in the Pacific Ocean

**Enclave**
A territory or region

**Endemic**
Native; found in a particular place

**Filter feeders**
Animals that feed on matter and particles found in water

**Germination**
Starting to grow

**Habitat**
The place where an animal makes its home

**Human encroachment**
Human beings settling and carrying out other activities in areas that were formerly natural

**Human subsistence farming**
Growing crops and rearing livestock to feed a family

**Indigenous**
Living or growing naturally in a particular place

**Initiative**
An idea to solve a problem or improve a situation

**Invertebrate**
An animal without a backbone

**Migratory**
Moving from one region or habitat to another, according to the seasons

**Oil palm plantations**
Areas of land where oil palm trees are grown and harvested

**Overwintering**
Spending the winter

**Parasitic disease**
An infectious disease caused or spread by a parasite

**Persecution**
Harassment or cruel treatment

**Poaching**
Hunting or catching an animal illegally

**Population trend**
The direction in which the population is changing, i.e. upwards or downwards

**Predation**
One animal killing and eating another

**Range**
The part of the world an animal inhabits

**Reintroduction**
Putting a species back into its former habitat

**Reticulated**
A pattern of lines that forms a net or web

**Roadkill**
An animal killed on the road by a vehicle

**Slash-and-burn agriculture**
Cutting and burning plants to make space for crops to be grown

**Sport hunting (also known as trophy hunting)**
Paying to hunt and kill an animal for fun (When very carefully managed, sport hunting can be used as a conservation tool to help threatened species and their habitats.)

**Sustainability (sustainable)**
Using natural resources in a way that we could keep doing for a long time

**Symbiosis (symbiotic)**
The close relationship between two species

**Wildlife trade**
The sale or exchange of wild animals and plants by people (includes live animals and plants, and animal and plant products)

# Acknowledgments

Huge thanks go to the team at the People's Trust for Endangered Species (PTES) for their collaboration on The 100 Day Project. I have learnt so much about the creatures and habitats that they and their partners protect. I am grateful, too, for the encouragement and expertise of Button Books, turning my words and illustrations into a fully formed book.

I would also like to thank Brett Westwood, an incredible naturalist and inspiring author and broadcaster, for agreeing to step into this book.

Finally, I'd like to pay tribute to all the people helping to ensure that these 100 species, and many hundreds more, are part of the world for future generations.

First published 2021 by Guild of Master Craftsman Publications Ltd, Castle Place, 166 High Street, Lewes, East Sussex BN7 1XU, UK. Text & illustrations © Rachel Hudson 2021. Copyright in the Work © GMC Publications Ltd, 2021. ISBN 978 1 78708 105 5. Distributed by Publishers Group West in the United States. All rights reserved. The right of Rachel Hudson to be identified as the author of this work has been asserted in accordance with the Copyright, Designs and Patents Act 1988, sections 77 and 78. No part of this publication may be reproduced, stored in a retrieval system or transmitted in any form or by any means without the prior permission of the publisher and copyright owner. This book is sold subject to the condition that all designs are copyright and are not for commercial reproduction without the permission of the designer and copyright owner. While every effort has been made to obtain permission from the copy right holders for all material used in this book, the publishers willbe pleased to hear from anyone who has not been appropriately acknowledged and to make the correction in future reprints. The publishers and author can accept no legal responsibility for any consequences arising from the application of information, advice or instructions given in this publication. A catalog record for this book is available from the British Library. Publisher: Jonathan Bailey · Production Manager: Jim Bulley · Designer: Robin Shields · Editor: Laura Paton Color origination by GMC Reprographics. Printed and bound in China.

The website addresses included in this book were valid at the time of going to press. However, it is possible that contents or addresses may have changed since the publication of this book. No responsibility for any such changes can be accepted by either the author or the publisher.

Button Books